Penguin Reference Books

**The Penguin
Shorter Atlas of the Bible**

L. H. Grollenberg was born in 1916
and entered the Dominican Order
in 1934. He is an experienced
archaeologist and has a first-hand
acquaintance with the lands of the
Bible.

Luc. H. Grollenberg

Translated by Mary F. Hedlund, M.A. (Oxon)

Penguin Books

The Penguin
Shorter Atlas of the Bible

Penguin Books Ltd, Harmondsworth, Middlesex, England
Penguin Books, 40 West 23rd Street, New York, New York 10010, U.S.A.
Penguin Books Australia Ltd, Ringwood, Victoria, Australia
Penguin Books Canada Ltd, 2801 John Street, Markham, Ontario, Canada L3R 1B4
Penguin Books (N.Z.) Ltd, 182–190 Wairau Road, Auckland 10, New Zealand

Kleine Atlas de Bijbel first published 1959
This translation first published under the title *Shorter Atlas of the Bible* by
Thomas Nelson & Sons 1959
Published simultaneously in Penguin Books and Allen Lane under the title
The Penguin Shorter Atlas of the Bible 1978
Reprinted 1983, 1984

Contents

List of Maps   7
Foreword   9
Publisher's Note to the Penguin Edition   11
Abbreviations   12

The Background

A Strip of Land between Sea and Desert   15
Meeting Place of Many Cultures   22
Reconnaissance in Palestine   37
Remnants of Ancient Civilizations   43
Excavation of Tells and Tombs   51
Deciphering the Ancient Tongues   61
The Technique of Biblical Geography   75

The Old Testament

The Chronicles of the Old Testament   82
The Patriarchs   89
Exodus from the House of Bondage   103
Settlement in Canaan   111
From Joshua to Saul   120
Jerusalem – City of David and of God   129
Judah and Israel   148

In the Hands of the Assyrians   153
The Prophets   163
Exile and Return   173
The Jews in the Hellenistic World   183

The New Testament

Under the Roman Eagle   191
Voices in the Wilderness   199
The Hireling and the Good Shepherd   213
The Gospels: Background and Composition   215
Jesus of Nazareth   223
'My Witnesses to the End of the Earth'   237

Acknowledgements   245
Indexes   248

List of Maps

1   In the Heart of the Ancient World: The rulers of Palestine during Biblical times
2   Palestine: Geographical survey showing the most important excavations
3   The Wanderings of the Patriarchs
4   Campaigns of Joshua and the Judges
5   Jerusalem in the time of Christ
6   From Saul to the Exile: The time of the Kings
7   The Expansion of Assyria
8   The Persian Empire and the Expeditions of Alexander the Great
9   Palestine in the Gospels and Acts
10 The Travels of Saint Paul according to the Acts of the Apostles

Foreword

This *Shorter Atlas of the Bible* is an attempt to present in small compass a picture of the world in which the books of the Bible found their origin. It is not simply a shortened version of the *Atlas of the Bible*. The material has been designed anew, on the same principles, using maps, a large number of illustrations, and a short text to link them; but it has been designed to suit the smaller format and to provide as much as possible for as low a price as possible. Naturally, this has meant some limitations.

First, the maps: these are confined to the key periods and show only the most important places. Those readers who seek more detailed information are referred to the larger *Atlas*, the Index of which contains virtually every geographical name in the Bible.

Again, the illustrations are fewer than in the larger work. Consequently, the selection has been to some extent revised, partly for didactic reasons, partly for reasons of printing technique, and finally because archaeologists have not been idle during the past four years and therefore something of their activities and discoveries had to be presented.

To make the best use of space and layout, the text is divided into short chapters, in which occasionally sketch maps and tables are inserted to clarify certain points. Brief references to relevant photographs in other parts of the book have been included. A further aim was to produce a pleasantly readable text. Lastly, the use of this *Atlas* in schools was considered, with the understanding that to the teacher would fall the lot of explaining more fully the unavoidably compressed accounts that are given.

What this *Shorter Atlas of the Bible* has to offer in the three fields of cartography, illustration, and text is naturally a limited selection from an abundance of material. That other selections were possible and equally to be defended, no one is more aware than the author himself. Often hesitating, he was helped to a decision by a deep conviction which, though it is nowhere explicitly formulated in the text, the reader is likely now and then to perceive. This is the conviction, first, that Israel alone of all the peoples of the world came in the course of the ages to an appreciation of God which implied a coherent interpretation of the mysteries of mankind; and, secondly, that the life, death, and resurrection of Jesus of Nazareth open the way for all men to a complete development of their human existence. The author has ventured to place before the public this attempt at a realistic approach to the lands of the Bible, in the hope that someone may by its means become more familiar with the Book of Books, and thus make his own something of that way of life which is able to make men happy.

Thanks are here expressed to the translator, Miss Hedlund, and to Fr Mark Schoof, O.P., for his careful and intelligent co-operation in the correction of the proofs.

Luc. Grollenberg O.P.

Jerusalem,
September 1959

Publisher's Note to the Penguin Edition

In this reissue of the popular Nelson English-language 1959 edition we have changed only the arrangement of illustrations and notes (to make these more convenient for the reader); we have corrected a few minor errors and added metric equivalents for dimensions, weights, and altitudes.

Abbreviations

Old Testament

Gn	– Genesis
Ex	– Exodus
Lv	– Leviticus
Num	– Numbers
Dt	– Deuteronomy
Jos	– Joshua
Jg	– Judges
2 S	– 2 Samuel
1 K, 2 K	– 1 and 2 Kings
1 Ch, 2 Ch	– 1 and 2 Chronicles
Ezr	– Ezra
Neh	– Nehemiah
Ps	– Psalms
Pr	– Proverbs
Is	– Isaiah
Jer	– Jeremiah
Ezk	– Ezekiel
Dn	– Daniel
Am	– Amos
2 Mac	– 2 Maccabees

New Testament

Mt	– Matthew
Mk	– Mark
Lk	– Luke
Jn	– John
Ac	– Acts
Ro	– Romans
1 Co, 2 Co	– 1 and 2 Corinthians
Gal	– Galatians
Eph	– Ephesians
Ph	– Philippians
Col	– Colossians
1 and 2 Thess	– 1 and 2 Thessalonians
1 and 2 Ti	– 1 and 2 Timothy
Tit	– Titus
Philem	– Philemon
1, 2, 3 Ep of Jn	– 1, 2, and 3 John
Rev	– Revelation

c.	– circa
cf.	– compare
Ch.	– Chapter
T.	– Tell

The spelling of Biblical names in this book is usually that of the Revised Standard Version of the Bible.

For Arabic names the English system of transliteration has been used.

Nihil Obstat:

Thomas Hanlon, L.S.S., S.T.L., Censor Deputatus

Die 14 Octobris 1959

Imprimatur:

✠ Gordon Joseph, Archbishop of St Andrews and Edinburgh

Die 14 Octobris 1959

A Strip of Land between Sea and Desert

A nation's development is largely determined by the nature of the soil upon which it lives, the climate of its country, and the means of communication with other inhabited areas. The ancient nation of Israel was no exception to this rule. In so far as the Bible reflects the cultural and spiritual development of Israel, an intelligent understanding of the Bible demands some knowledge of geographical data. As far as Palestine is concerned these data are very interesting. The map of this land, so easy to draw with its simple lines of Jordan valley and coast, is reproduced on a small scale in Map 1 against the background of a much larger region which includes no less than five seas.

One should begin here by noting two things. The first is the character of the Syrian or Syro-Arabian desert east of Palestine, an endless, stony steppe, about 600 metres (2,000 ft) above sea-level, where the rain from the west scarcely penetrates and where there are few oases. Until the advent of motorized transport this desert country made direct traffic between Palestine (with Egypt lying behind) and the region round the Persian Gulf impossible. Even for the camel, the one-humped species which came into use during the second millennium B.C., large sections of this steppe are scarcely passable, above all the basalt region south-east of Damascus (cf. Figure 2, p. 23). For although the camel can go for days without water and store a provision of food in its hump which can, if necessary, be supplemented by dry grass and thistles, its hoofs are made for sandy ground and it moves with difficulty over rough stones and loose gravel. The route from Jerusalem to Babylon, 860 kilometres (537 miles) apart as the

15

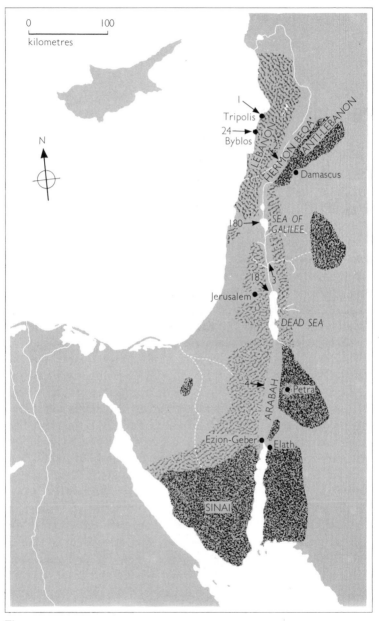

Figure 1

Plate 1. The port of Tripolis, an ancient Phoenician settlement where Arvad. Tyre, and Sidon each had their quarter, hence the Greek name 'triple city'. In the background the Lebanon.

crow flies, led first north-eastwards, a long way past Damascus, and then farther along the Euphrates in a south-easterly direction, a journey of roughly 1,250 km (780 miles). Cut off to the east by the Syrian Desert and west by a coast which offered little anchorage to sea traffic, Palestine could only be reached from the north and, less easily, from the south. This north-south orientation is intensified by the second peculiarity revealed by the map and to which the attention of the reader is drawn. The map of Palestine is dominated by the vertical line of the Jordan valley which links two inland seas. This valley is considered the deepest in the world. The surface of the Sea of Galilee lies 212 metres (700 ft) lower than the level of the Mediterranean Sea; that of the

Plate 2. Mount Hermon seen from the NE from the slopes of the Lebanon across the Beqa'.

Dead Sea is 392 metres (1,290 ft) lower, and the Dead Sea is up to 400 metres (1,311 ft) deep. As a cross-section of Palestine at the level of Bethlehem shows (see Figure 3, p. 37), the surface of the desert appears to rise slightly and then suddenly dips down into the Jordan valley. It rises again to the west and then slopes gradually towards the coast. The relief of Palestine proper will be discussed later. Suffice it to remark here that this subsidence is not confined to Palestine. Figure 1 shows that it continues south of the Dead Sea in a valley 170 km (106 miles) long, called in the Bible the Arabah, and is carried on near the small town of 'Aqaba, close to the ruins of the Biblical Elath, by a side-branch of the Red Sea. This valley also appears to continue north of

Palestine. Figure 1 suggests a similar sort of relief: the level of the desert first rises and forms Mount Hermon, continued north through the Anti-Lebanon; then follows a valley called the Beqa' (an Arabic word for valley), after which the level rises again to form the Lebanon. As can be seen on Map 3 the Orontes rises in the Beqa' and then flows northwards parallel to the coast. This points to a further continuation of the great north-south depression. Yet although this region resembles Palestine in the essential features of its ground relief, there are also considerable differences. The mountains on either side of the depression are very much higher. Moreover, the Beqa', although it appears to be a continuation of the Jordan valley, is in reality separated from it by a piece of mountainous land. All these factors make it easy to understand how in antiquity the Lebanon and Palestine could be classed together under the name Canaan, while, on the other hand, the inhabitants of Palestine could at a certain period form a cultural and political unit.

The numbers on Figure 1 are those of the photographs in which the regions mentioned are shown: in the north the old Phoenician trading city of Tripolis (see Plate 1); in the background the snow-covered Lebanon (the root *lbn* means 'to be white'). To the south, where the plain narrows considerably between the mountains and the sea, is Byblos (Plate 24). Then comes a view across the wide Beqa' to the majestic Hermon (Plate 2), whose name is derived from *hrm*, sacred, unassailable. Next a picture of the Sea of Galilee (Plate 180) with Tiberias in the foreground and in the distance the Transjordan highlands. The photograph of the Jordan valley (Plate 3), taken from a very great height in a north-north-westerly direction, includes the lake in the hazy background, upper right. The dark ribbon running from there to the lower left is the dense undergrowth called in the Bible the 'pride' of the Jordan, inhabited in ancient times by so many animals that only the daring risked showing themselves there (cf. Jer 12.5). The rapidly flowing Jordan covers the 109 km (68 miles) from the Sea of Galilee to the Dead Sea (Plate 18) with so many twists and turns that its length is reckoned at 320 km

Plate 4. Part of the desolate Negeb, the south country, looking east. In the distance, the valley of the Arabah running from north to south; behind, the highlands of the Edomites.

(200 miles)! Finally, there is an aerial photo of the Arabah (Plate 4) with the desolate landscape of the Negeb in the foreground and, across the valley, the highlands. There, in the dark strip, lie the ruins of the famous 'rose red' city of Petra (Plates 150–52).

Plate 3. The Jordan valley from a considerable height, looking NNW. To the right the valley of the Jabbok joins the Jordan valley proper. The latter shows dark on the photograph because of the dense undergrowth through which the river flows. The light patch a little to the left of the Jabbok mouth is *Tell ed-Dâmiyeh*, the tell of the city of Adam, where the waters of the Jordan were held back (Jos 3.16). The side valley on the left is the *Wâdi Far'ah*. At its head lies the tell of ancient Tirzah (see Plate 119, taken from the opposite direction).

21

Meeting Place of Many Cultures

Accessible only from the north and south the coastal region formed the natural link between the two most important cultural regions of antiquity, Egypt and Mesopotamia. According to the ancient Egyptians themselves, their land consisted of two parts (1 and 2 on Figure 2): the Nile valley proper, many hundreds of miles long and in most places 15 to 30 km (10 to 18 miles) wide, flanked by sun-scorched deserts (Plate 5), and the broad fan-shaped Delta with sides of about 200 km (120 miles) long. Agriculture depended entirely upon the annual flooding of the Nile, and only the well organized effort of all the inhabitants could turn it to advantage.

The earliest known Pharaoh, Menes, had already united the 'Two Lands' into one strong state. Both he and his earliest successors, who ruled from the magnificent and now completely vanished city of Memphis (Plate 6), just south of Cairo, and the later Pharaohs who had their court in Thebes, 600 km (375 miles) to the south (Plates 7–9), wore a double crown, that of Upper and Lower Egypt. On the sides of their thrones especially they liked to have a symmetrical 'vignette' showing two Nile gods binding the papyrus reed of the Delta and the lotus of the Nile valley to the hieroglyph which expressed the concept of union (Plate 51). In the isolation of their country surrounded by desert, the Egyptians, conservative by nature, were able to preserve for three thousand years, without any essential changes, the first flowering of their astonishing culture. Their fertile soil, however, did not supply all their needs. They had no wood suitable for the build-ing of houses and ships. From the very earliest times Egyptian

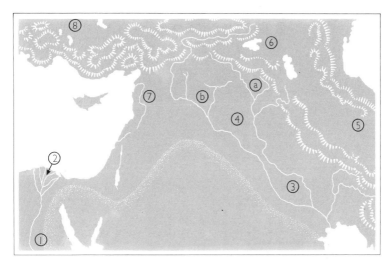

Figure 2

Plate 5. The Nile somewhere between Cairo and Luxor. Note the sharp difference between the irrigated region and the sun-baked desert on either side of it.

23

Plate 6. The oldest capital of Egypt, a little south of Cairo, was called *mn-nfr* on account of its beauty. The inhabitants of Israel shortened this to Moph or Noph, and the Greeks called it Memphis. Behind the palms which now grow where the city formerly stood, one sees on the edge of the western desert the famous stepped pyramid of the Pharaoh Zoser, *c.* 2600 B.C.

Plate 7. The Nile near Luxor. The small town derives its name from the ruins of the 'city of Amon' (No-Amon or No in the Bible, called Thebes by the Greeks) among which it is built and which the Arabian inhabitants called *el-Quṣûr*, 'the castles'. A little farther north lies the small town of Karnak, near the ruins of the Amon temple. In the centre of the photograph, on the near bank, can be seen the great rows of columns of Rameses II, shown in close-up in Plate 73. On the west bank an arrow indicates the Valley of the Kings. Here Hatshepsut built her Temple of the Dead.

Plate 8. The famous Valley of the Kings. Left of the centre, a dotted line indicates the spot where the processions entered the desolate valley. Every pharaoh of the New Kingdom had his burial chamber hewn in the heart of the mountains, which thus served as pyramids. Of the 60 known tombs, each reached by a long and often magnificently decorated corridor from the valley, three are visible on the photograph: near 1, the entrance of the long shaft to the tomb of Rameses II; near 2, that of Rameses VI; near 3 begins the passage to the tomb of Tutankhamon, the only one that escaped the attention of tomb robbers of former centuries. It was found almost intact in 1922 after years of searching by scholars who knew that it had probably remained untouched.

Plate 9. In the foreground the Temple of the Dead of Queen Hatshepsut, with three ascending terraces, of which the second is the largest. In the background is a much older temple from *c.* 2000 B.C., with only one terrace.

Plate 10. Obelisks in an excavated temple at Byblos, testifying to Egyptian influence in this city.

Plate 11. The most famous of the rare plantations of cedars remaining in the Lebanon. It lies 30 kilometres (20 miles) SE of Tripolis and contains about 400 trees, some of which are more than 1,000 years old.

Plate 12. At the edge of the cedar wood.

traders sailed along the coast of Palestine to the Phoenician ports at the foot of the Lebanon, there to barter the products of their own country for lofty cedar trunks. In this way Byblos, for example, became almost an Egyptian city (see Plates 10 and 24 and p. 45). Later Pharaohs thought it worth while to undertake the wearying desert journey along the coast (170 km – 106 miles – from Pelusium to Raphia; see Figure 7, p. 182) to occupy Canaan with their armies and obtain the precious cedar wood by force (Plates 11–13). Canaan had thus been in the power and under the influence of Egypt for some centuries before the Israelites settled there. As the latter expressed it, Canaan was a brother of Egypt and a son of Ham (cf. Gn 10.6). Their military expeditions sometimes carried the men of Thebes to the banks of the Euphrates, and every time they saw it they stood and stared. Here the world was completely topsy-turvy: a real river, almost as wide as their own Nile but flowing from north to south! Little did they realize that this 'backward-flowing' stream had, together with the Tigris, made possible the development of civilizations at least as old and as varied as their own, yet completely different.

Mesopotamia is also made up of two parts (3 and 4 on Figure 2). The southern region is flat and can, if proper advantage be taken of the annual floods, be made extremely fertile. Here, shortly after 3000 B.C., flourished the Sumerian city states such as Ur, Lagash, and Nippur. North of the point where the two rivers are closest, where Baghdad now stands on the Tigris (see Map 1), with, 80 km (50 miles) to the south, the ruins of Babylon near the Euphrates, the two rivers diverge and are separated by as much as 550 km (340 miles) of steppe-like plains. The homeland of the Assyrians (near *a*) lay on the Tigris, between Cizre, where the river emerges from the upper region of the mountains (Plate 14), and the two tributaries which are now called the Great and Little Zab. On the Euphrates, flowing far to the west, mighty cities and states flourished and decayed. Among them was Mari (Plate 15),

Plate 13. Conquered Phoenicians cutting cedars for the Pharaoh. Right, four of the vanquished humble themselves before an Egyptian officer (not shown). Detail from a relief carved on a temple wall in Thebes (Karnak) by order of Seti I (1317–1301 B.C.).

80 km (50 miles) south of the place where the Khâbûr, the Habor of the Bible, flows into the Euphrates to the right of *b*.

Geographically, Mesopotamia was not nearly so isolated as Egypt. The two main rivers, much more capricious than the Nile, could suddenly overflow in southern Mesopotamia and sweep away the work of generations. It is not by chance that the earliest known version of the story of the Flood originated in this region. Sometimes, too, tribes from the northern highlands of Iran (5) and Armenia (6) and nomads from the Arabian peninsula, attracted by the riches of civilization, poured into the regions along the Tigris and Euphrates and thus enriched the existing cultures with new elements. Whenever a power of any importance arose in Mesopotamia it automatically pressed westwards, where the Euphrates is no more than 200 km (125 miles) from the coast, which can then be gained fairly easily. For this region (around 7 on Figure 2), roughly corresponding to the modern states of Syria and Lebanon, was particularly attractive to Mesopotamian powers, not only as a jumping-off ground for expansion towards wealthy Egypt, not only on account of the fertile hinterland and the cedars of Lebanon, but also because of the Phoenician trading centres on the sea coast with its many bays. On Map 3 some of these trading centres are shown: the great city of Ugarit, destroyed *c*. 1200 B.C. by the so-called Peoples of the Sea and

Plate 14. The Tigris near *Jezîret Ibn Omar*, the ancient Bezabde, where Alexander the Great crossed the river twelve days before his decisive victory over the Persians near Gaugamela (2 October 331 B.C.). At that time the Tigris flowed around the city at high tide, hence the alternative name of Gozarta, 'island' (Arabic *jezîreh*). For a time the city was ruled by the chief Ibn Omar. Since 1929 the Turkish frontier, visible in the background, has run in front of the city with its ancient ramparts. Its Turkish name is Cizre.

Plate 15. Mari on the Euphrates, for many centuries a flourishing trading centre, destroyed *c*. 1700 B.C. by Hammurabi, and accidentally discovered in 1933 by nomads who upturned a statue while digging a grave. It has subsequently been excavated in annual campaigns. The photograph, taken after the fourth campaign, shows in the background the famous royal palace with its 260 rooms, inner courts, etc. A collection of roughly 2,000 tablets with cuneiform writing was found, providing valuable information concerning the history and culture of this region. In the distance, the Euphrates.

accidentally discovered in 1927 in the mound of *Râs Shamra*. Excavation of this tell still continues to provide valuable information concerning the ancient culture of Canaan. There was also the island city of Arvad (Plate 16), the already mentioned towns of Tripolis and Byblos, Sidon, and finally Tyre (Plate 17). From the very earliest times the seafaring inhabitants of these cities carried on commercial relations with the western world, with the copper island of Cyprus, with the coasts of Asia Minor, and with the Greek archipelago. If one bears in mind that the northern part of the coastal region was strongly influenced by the Hittites of Asia Minor (8) it is obvious that one may indeed justifiably speak of this land as a meeting place of many cultures.

Plate 16. The island of Ruâd, 3 km (2 miles) from the Phoenician coast. The important city of Arvad was situated here.

Plate 17. Tyre, once a mighty island city like Arvad, was taken by Alexander in 332 B.C. after a siege of seven months, with the help of a causeway which linked the city permanently with the mainland and transformed it into a peninsula.

Plate 18. The Dead Sea from a great height, looking SSE. The dotted line indicates roughly the area shown in Plate 159. From the Jordan and smaller rivers like the Arnon this inland sea receives over 6 million tonnes of water per day. In normal conditions this would mean that the water would rise about a centimetre (half an inch) every day, but the rapid evaporation in this hot, deep bowl between high rock walls prevents this. Because of the evaporation the water is very rich in minerals; it contains roughly 25 per cent of salts; see the pans for extracting salt near the Jordan estuary to the left. Fish brought down to the Dead Sea die within a few seconds. Called in the Bible the Salt Sea or Sea of the Plain, it was given the name of Dead Sea at the beginning of our era; only a miraculous stream flowing from God's Temple could render the water capable of sustaining life (Ezk 47.1–12).

Reconnaissance in Palestine

Map 1 shows a bird's-eye view of Palestine, lying between five seas and on the only passable road linking Africa and Asia. On Map 2 we see the country on a larger scale. It is divided into two unequal parts by a green strip – the deep valley through which the Jordan flows to the Dead Sea, the most remarkable of all lakes (Plate 18). Here are a few short remarks concerning the country west of the Jordan valley. The colours show that the central chain of hills in the southern part, roughly between Hebron and Baal-hazor, is fairly high and massive (cf. the section in Figure 3, level with Bethlehem; the sketch of the earth layers suggests that the region round the Dead Sea in particular is a paradise for geologists!). Farther north, where the central chain of mountains formerly bore the name of Ephraim, it descends and is often broken up by valleys. Near Shechem it is even transversed by a narrow cleft. The mountain to the south was called Mount Gerizim, that to the north Mount Ebal, and between these two massive peaks lay ancient Shechem (Plates 66–7). Alongside the two mountains, on the eastern side, lies a narrow fertile plain which, when our photograph was taken, at the beginning of June, was 'white for harvest' (Plate 65). A little farther, past ancient Tirzah, after which a wide vale opens on to the valley of the

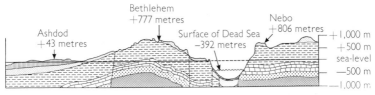

Figure 3

Jordan (Plate 119), the mountain country seems to divide: one half runs north-west, ending in Mount Carmel which descends steeply into the sea (Plate 128), the other north-east, where the crescent-shaped mountain barrier of Gilboa bounds the plain of Jezreel (Plate 94). From Megiddo one looks across the plain to where the central mountain range begins again in Lower Galilee (Plate 88; cf. Plate 19, from the top of Mount Tabor). There lies Nazareth and, a little farther north, *Kafr Kenna* (Plate 20).

The coastal plain, protected over most of its length by a line of dunes, is very broad in the south where once the Philistines lived. After Joppa (Jaffa) comes the much narrower plain of Sharon, marshy, since the dunes prevent the water from draining off, and mentioned in the Bible for its impenetrable and luxuriant vegetation. On the right-hand side of Map 2, one sees how the highlands east of the Jordan valley are divided into four by the deep clefts of the Yarmuk (not mentioned in the Bible), the Jabbok (Plate 63; cf. Plate 3), and the Arnon (Plate 80).

After this rapid glance at the ground relief, two other closely related factors must be taken into consideration: the rainfall distribution and the position of the natural trade routes. During the summer, from mid-May until mid-September, there is no rain at all in Palestine. The dew, however, is sometimes very heavy and of real importance for agriculture. The rainfall during the remaining months, of which the first and last showers ('the early and later rains', Dt 11.14, etc.) are so indispensable for good harvests, comes from above the Mediterranean and is naturally heavier in the northern part of Palestine than in the south, where the coastline begins to curve towards the west. In addition, the central mountain chain attracts most rain where it is highest. This means that the mountains of Judaea and also the hills to the west (called by the Judaeans the Lowland) catch most of the rain,

Plate 19. From the towers of the basilica which crowns Mount Tabor (see Plate 89) one sees to the west, over the Greek monastery and its annexes, the hills of Lower Galilee, where Nazareth lies hidden.

Plate 20. View of *Kafr Kenna*, a picturesque spot a few miles NE of Nazareth, considered since the fourth century to be the Cana of John 2.1.

while the east side, the Wilderness of Judaea (Plate 21), lies within the 'rain shadow' and receives very little. The same is true of the deep and tropically hot Jordan valley. Towards the north, where the mountain chain becomes lower and more broken up, the rain can penetrate farther east. This part of the Jordan valley is thus better suited for agriculture, since it also possesses many springs and brooklets. The steeply rising edge of the district east of the Jordan receives a heavier precipitation throughout its entire length.

The route followed by the main roads is also determined by the relief of the country. As can be seen from the dotted lines on Map 2, only two main traffic roads are possible in the south, both running north to south, one along the coast and the other along the central mountain chain. Quite a number of Israelite cities lay along this road, and the modern asphalt road from Hebron to Shechem follows the same route. Anyone driving reflectively along it on a clear day can see on his left the Mediterranean sparkling behind the coastal plain with its row of dunes, and on his right the edge of the Transjordan highland. If he takes the trouble to climb a high peak, like *Nebi Samwîl* near Gibeon (Plate 83), he will be able to see both boundaries and marvel at the wonderful structure of this Holy Land.

Past Shechem the situation becomes less easy to survey. The plain of Jezreel, joining the coastal plain in the north-west at the bay of Acco and running east to Beth-shan, offers here the only possibility of easy communication between east and west. In addition, the bulk of Mount Carmel forces the coastal road (the main road from Egypt to Mesopotamia!) to curve in a north-

Plate 21. The wilderness of Judaea at the level of Bethlehem. In the distance, the Dead Sea; behind, the mountains of Moab.

Plate 22. The fortress, exactly in the middle of Plate 21, stands near the tower shown upper right in this photograph. They form part of the wall surrounding the monastery, built here against the side of the deeply indented Kidron valley by followers of Sabas, a Cappadocian who came here as a hermit in 478. Throughout the following centuries this monastery was famous as a centre of art and learning.

Plate 23. The hill country of Judaea.

easterly direction, through the pass which emerges on to the plain near Megiddo and there to cross the road running from west to east.

This rapid survey makes it clear how much the situation of the northern tribes of Israel differed from that of the tribe of Judah, who lived rather isolated in their hilly (see Plate 23) yet compact and clearly defined highland. It was not by chance that four successive kings had their capitals here, at Shechem, Penuel, Tirzah and Samaria. Life was easier for the northern Israelites in their more fertile and well-watered land. They mingled unobtrusively with the Canaanites who had stayed on the fertile plains of Jezreel, Acco, and Beth-shan, and had varied contacts with the Phoenicians of Tyre and Sidon and the Aramaic states in the north-east. In this flourishing, open country they were perhaps an easy prey for pagan conquest and influence. On the other hand, their descendants in Jesus' time were readier to accept His preaching of the Kingdom.

Remnants of Ancient Civilizations

The entire region so far discussed, that is Palestine, Syria, and Egypt on the one hand, and Mesopotamia on the other, is studded with ruins from the past. Some still rise high above the landscape, others have been buried for centuries beneath sand and silt. The ancient Egyptians built their simple houses of mud bricks (Plates 75–6), not a very durable material. For this reason scarcely anything remains of great cities like Memphis, and palms now grow where houses once stood (Plate 6). But for their 'eternal homes', as they called their tombs, and for the temples of their gods, they used either blocks of natural stone, found in abundance in the desert on either side of their land, or else hard granite from Elephantine (Plate 140) and regions farther south. This they fashioned and transported with the most amazing skill. The fact that they used this stone accounts for the numerous visible ruins in Egypt. Admittedly they were often partly buried during the course of time under Nile silt and drifting sand (see for example the difference in colour on the pillars at Luxor, Plate 73), but this helped to preserve many precious reliefs, like those on top of a fallen obelisk in Karnak (Plate 42), and even whole buildings, like the magnificent temple at Edfu (Plate 146).

In Mesopotamia, however, there was scarcely any stone suitable for building. The inhabitants mostly used bricks baked in the sun or in a fire, with bitumen for mortar (Gn 11.3). Centuries of rain storms and floods reduced these ancient cities to shapeless heaps of clay. Only the remains of the temple towers (called ziggurats) still rise here and there above the wide plain. These were enormous constructions which the people built in order to

draw closer to the gods, or, rather, to offer the gods a ladder down which they could climb to the earth (Plate 60).

Syria and Palestine contain ruins of all kinds and of every century. Sometimes a whole series of successive cultures is represented on one spot. One example is Byblos (Plate 24). In the foreground is the Mediterranean Sea; behind the narrow, fertile coastal plain is the beginning of the Lebanon flank which rises to about 3,000 metres (9,000 ft) above sea-level. The village to the left is called *Jebeil* and thus retains the old name which the Assyrians spelled Gubla and the Israelites Gebal. The inhabitants were known as wood-workers (1 K 5.18) and shipbuilders (Ezk 27.9). This is understandable as they had little space for agriculture or cattle breeding but had immense cedar woods behind them and a coast with many sheltered bays in front of them. The church in the centre of the village (in circle 1) was built by the Crusaders who occupied Giblet, as they called it, from 1104 to 1188, and after that from 1198 until a stormy night in 1266, when the last defenders escaped from the superior besiegers of Sultan Baibars across the sea to Tripolis. The church, with its magnificent baptistery, is in pure Romanesque style. The fort, of which the keep can be seen (in circle 2), dates from the same period. The amphitheatre (in circle 3) is Roman and fully a thousand years older. At this time the slopes of the Lebanon were already largely denuded of their cedars, but Byblos, as it was pronounced in those days, continued to flourish thanks to the cult of Adonis, whose myth was localized in the neighbourhood. Two thousand years older again than the amphitheatre is the temple (in circle 4) with its many obelisks (seen in close-up in Plate 10).

As early as 3000 B.C. Egyptian merchants visited this town, already famous as a religious centre, and incorporated it into their legends about Isis and Osiris. Yet what they were really seeking in this land of gods was cedar wood. They received the precious trunks mainly in exchange for the writing material which they made from the papyrus reeds of their Delta. The Greek world obtained these sheets of papyrus from Byblos and it was thus that

Plate 24. The small village of *Jebeil* and the excavated tell of ancient Byblos.

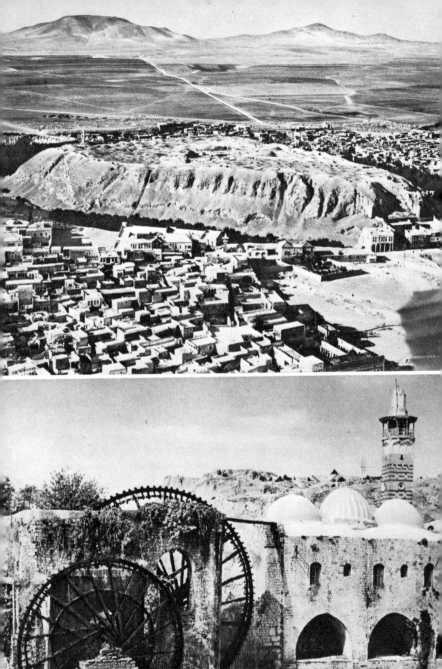

a book, in Greek, came to be called *biblion*, from which is derived, via the Latin *biblia*, our word *Bible*, the book par excellence. The Greeks also adopted the writing system of the Phoenicians who, after centuries of experiment (the development is not yet completely clear), had succeeded, long before 1000 B.C., in simplifying the old complicated method of writing into an alphabet. To the right of the house in the foreground, used by the excavators as a workshop and storage place, one can see the foundations of houses built *c.* 4000 B.C. Counting from the medieval church and fort, this photo thus shows remains dating over a period of more than fifty centuries. One must bear in mind that the Roman amphitheatre was only revealed by excavation; it even owes its present site to the diggers, who moved it because they wanted to continue excavating the original site. The same is true of the temple in circle 4. All these investigations were possible because the village of Jebeil and the Giblet of the Crusaders were built beside the ruins of ancient Gubla/Byblos and not on top of them.

Happily for the archaeologists this also happened in other places, such as the town of Hama on the Orontes (Plate 25), picturesquely situated about the tell of the ancient city which appears in the Bible as Hamath. This tell is so high that it rises above the white domes of the buildings and the musically creaking paddle-wheels which convey part of the river water to high aqueducts (Plate 26). The height of the tell is due to the fact that Hamath was destroyed and rebuilt many times.

The houses in these regions were not very solidly built. The walls were usually made of two rows of rough stones. The cavity was filled with pebbles and the outside smeared with mud. Sometimes the upper part of the wall was made of bricks of sun-baked clay. The flat roof rested on light beams, and more earth was smeared on top. When a town was destroyed only the lower part of the walls remained standing; the spaces in between became filled up with the materials of the upper structure. The

Plate 25. The tell of ancient Hamath surrounded by the houses of modern Hama.

Plate 26. The Orontes in Hama. The tell stands in the background.

inhabitants, those who had not been put to the sword or died of plague or starvation, departed. Wind and rain flattened everything to a mound of earth. Such a mound was already called a tell in the oldest Semitic languages. Drawn by the attractive site, people then came years later to live on this spot. As Jeremiah expressed it, 'the city shall be rebuilt on its mound' (Jer 30.18). With every succeeding destruction the mound rose higher. Turning now from the tell of Hama, the following chapter will deal with the investigation of tells in Palestine.

Plate 27. Remains of the fortress of Machaerus, restored by Herod the Great. In the background, the Dead Sea, which lies 1,130 metres (3,700 ft) lower, and behind, the steep mountain wall of the desert of Judaea.

Plate 28. Across the small valley of *el-Buqeia* one sees the citadel of Hyrcanium, built by John Hyrcanus and fortified by Herod the Great. From his hermitage, a few miles farther west (Mar Saba; see Plate 22), Sabas founded in 492, in the ruins of this fortress, a monastery which flourished until the ninth century.

Plate 29. A view of Bethlehem looking SE. The arrow indicates the Herodium, the fortress which Herod built and intended as his tomb.

Excavation of Tells and Tombs

Where a tell consists of the accumulated remains of successively destroyed cities, the walls of a trench dug down through this mound should show as many layers as there were cities. Oddly enough, this simple principle was only discovered in 1890, although scholars had already been engaged for half a century in investigating the antiquities of Palestine. They had completely overlooked the numerous tells. In that year W. Flinders Petrie set out to examine a tell in the land of the Bible. Throughout the preceding ten years this young Englishman had rendered great service to archaeology by his meticulous examination of tells in the Nile Delta. He had, among other things, learned to appreciate the true importance of such apparent trifles as potsherds. In 1890 he dug a number of trenches through *Tell el-Hesy*, east of Gaza (for this and other place names see Map 2). He immediately distinguished a number of layers, noted that each contained its characteristic shards, and could even assign an approximate date to some of them, since they yielded objects which he was able to fit into the already established periods of ancient Egyptian history. In this manner Petrie laid the foundations for a completely new and very important development in Palestinian archaeology.

During the years that followed, up to the First World War, a number of other tells were investigated, those of Gezer, Gaza,

Plate 30. The tell of Biblical Dothan, shortly after the first excavations in 1953

Plate 31. The same tell from the side, scarcely recognizable as such. Left, nomad tents.

Taanach, Megiddo, Samaria, and Jericho, by archaeological societies of various countries. After the war, when Palestine had become British mandated territory, a second phase began. Many countries took part under the supervision of the excellent Department of Antiquities and worked in close contact with each other. This contact was made easier by the newly created road network. National unrest, followed by the Second World War, brought archaeological activity almost to a standstill. Now, we have entered upon the third phase, but in a land divided. The Archaeological Service of Israel is extremely active, not only in important undertakings, such as that at Hazor (see Plate 86), but also in numerous other places where digging during the course of house and road building has turned up interesting relics of the past. In Jordan all possible facilities have been afforded foreign teams. During the past few years excavations have been made at Dothan (Plates 30–31), Shechem (Plates 66–7), Tirzah (Plates 119 and 32–3), Jericho, *Khirbet Qumrân* (Plates 156–7), and in Transjordan at Dibon.

The ideal method of investigating a tell is, of course, to begin by completely uncovering the remains of the most recent city. These are removed in their turn and the remains of the preceding city are examined. This process is continued until the foundations of the earliest city are laid bare. Such a method, however, is usually far too costly. For although ancient cities were usually small in size, the uncovering of such an area requires a large number of labourers who, under the leadership of experienced foremen, would allow no detail to escape them. It also requires a trained staff of surveyors, photographers, and draughtsmen to record accurately any finds made. For, before proceeding to the following layer, the first must be removed, and with it all the evidence. It is thus imperative that a record should be made for scientific publications in which later generations may find every detail of the original situation, since destroyed. It is for this reason that archaeologists usually confine themselves to a partial

Plate 32. Excavators at work in Biblical Tirzah.

Plate 33. Exposed foundations of Tirzah.

Plate 34. Weather-beaten Phoenician sepulchral monuments near *Amrît*, a city on the coast founded by the inhabitants of Arvad (see Plate 16). These giant structures indicate the presence of burial chambers dug deep in the ground beneath. The monument to the right consists of a pedestal with lion figures at the corners, on which rests a cylindrical block, 7 metres (23 ft) high, made from a single piece of stone.

Plate 35. Palestinian pottery. *Left* and *foot*: the oil lamp in the various stages of its development. In the earliest times an ordinary round dish was filled with oil and the wick placed across the edge. Then the potters curved the edge to hold the wick in position. Later the curve became more pronounced and, with the gracefully sloping sides, formed a sort of lip. *Right*: six pots and jars. Particularly striking is the one on which is modelled a face with a large nose and a pointed beard (21 cm (8 in.) high, Hyksos period, from Jericho). Above and below, vessels from the Israelite period. The three specimens on the right date from the Middle Bronze Age (*c.* 2000–1600 B.C.); the lowest is Mycenaean in character and was probably imported.

54

excavation. Once a tell has been selected (not only historical but practical considerations play a role here – ease of access, water supply, the proximity of a village which can supply diggers, etc.) a trial ditch is usually dug at the edge of the tell (see our aerial photo of Dothan, Plate 30, taken in 1953 during the first campaign) and a spot is chosen which seems likely to yield something of particular interest, a city gate, a palace, or a temple. If more money can be raised for the actual excavation and for scientific publications besides those concerning the work in progress (anyone who obtains a licence to dig must undertake to publish a record of his finds), a new section can be broached (Plate 86).

Since Petrie's time and especially in the second period, the technique of exposing the layers and interpreting their contents has progressed considerably. This can be attributed in part to an increasingly accurate knowledge of the shapes and workmanship of the pottery made during the various periods of antiquity. The study of this pottery is of the greatest importance for dating a layer which is being excavated, and nowadays an experienced archaeologist is able to assess the age of a small fragment to

Plates 36–7. The jars and dishes in which the ancient inhabitants of Palestine placed food for their dead are often found almost intact. 36: a group of pottery dating from before 3000 B.C. 37: a find dating from roughly 1800 B.C.

Plate 38. People buried round a horse, probably from the Hyksos period, found near *Tell el-'Ajjûl* south of Gaza.

Plate 39. In 1952 burial places dating from the time of Christ were found on the Mount of Olives near 'Dominus Flevit'. A large number of 'ossuaria', stone chests containing the bones of those who had first lain in a burial chamber (see Plate 187), came to light. The name of the deceased is often inscribed on these chests, sometimes in Greek, sometimes in Aramaic. On the Mount of Olives were found the names of Jairus, Martha and Mary (see Plate 190), Simon Bar Jonah, Jesus, Salome, Philo of Cyrene.

Plate 40. Two sarcophagi: the upper is a limestone ossuarium from the time of Christ; the name reads 'Salome, the wife of Lazarus'; below, a sarcophagus of baked clay from the twelfth century B.C. found at Beth-shan. A face, ears, and arms are modelled on the lid. This type, also found in the Nile Delta and in the country of the Philistines, testifies to Egyptian influence in Canaan.

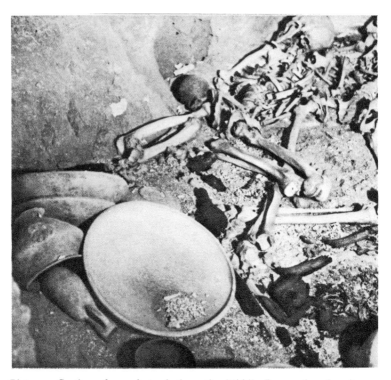

Plate 41. Section of a rock tomb from the Middle Bronze Age found near Jericho. The contents are now in the Rijksmuseum voor Oudheden in Leiden, arranged exactly as they were when found.

within a few centuries and that of a complete article to within a century. Along with a few typical pots and jars Plate 35 shows a series of oil lamps; the upper one dates from 2000 B.C. and the four below from the Graeco-Roman period.

Anyone excavating a tell always searches eagerly for the necropolis, the place or places in which the former inhabitants buried their dead. In the countries around Palestine the burial sites, at least those of any importance, were always indicated by a stone superstructure resembling those in Egypt (pyramids, mastabas), in some regions of Phoenicia (Plate 34), and in Petra (Plate 150). The ancient inhabitants of Palestine usually buried their dead in the natural caves in which their hilly country abounds, or hewed burial chambers from the soft sandstone. Those tombs which have remained intact are exceedingly difficult to find (otherwise they would have either been plundered or cleared for further use) and testify to a high level of culture, so far as one can judge from the funeral gifts. These finds vary enormously (Plates 36–40). In the Museum voor Oudheden in Leiden one may admire the contents of a rock tomb from Jericho dating from 1700 B.C. Everything is laid out exactly as it was found (Plate 41).

Teams of scholars from many countries, continually reinforced by enthusiastic young assistants, are collaborating in the examination of the land of Palestine. They are supported financially either by their own government or by some archaeological institution. In this manner we obtain each year a clearer picture of the daily life of the Israelites throughout the various periods of their history and also of that of their predecessors in this land, as far back as the prehistoric cave-dwellers.

Deciphering the Ancient Tongues

The examination of the ruins scattered about Egypt, Mesopotamia, and the Syria–Palestine coastal region would offer us no coherent picture of the early history of these lands if we were unable to read the texts found there. Happily we are able to do so thanks to some remarkable feats of linguistic skill, ranking with the greatest inventions of modern times.

Up to the beginning of the nineteenth century Egyptian hieroglyphs remained a mystery, although this puzzling writing was familiar enough. Since imperial times Rome had possessed a number of obelisks, enormous square columns with a pyramid-shaped top, always hewn from a single block. Some of these proud trophies from the land of the Pharaohs, where such pillars used to flank the temple doors, were covered on every side with hieroglyphs. In 1831 an obelisk was erected in Paris as a present from Mohamed Ali to the French king Louis-Philippe. As one can read on the base of this obelisk, in the Place de la Concorde, the civil engineer who arranged the transport was very pleased with the success of his undertaking. He did not know, apparently, that around 660 B.C. the Assyrians had conveyed two such obelisks from Thebes to Nineveh, a much longer and more difficult journey!

J. F. Champollion (1790–1832), who as a boy had listened breathlessly to stories of Napoleon's expedition in Egypt, felt it his vocation to resolve the mystery of the hieroglyphs. To this

Plate 42. Pyramid-shaped top of an obelisk in the ruins of the great temple of Amon at Thebes (Karnak).

end he studied Chinese, Arabic, Hebrew, Syriac, and above all Coptic, the language of the Egyptian Christians, and the only living link with the past. After fifteen years of dogged searching he found the first clue in 1822 and on his death, at the age of forty-two, he left behind him a grammar of ancient Egyptian in manuscript form. After him a number of able Egyptologists penetrated further into the mysteries of this language and from the numerous texts reconstructed the history of the ancient Egyptians and their admirable culture.

Hieroglyphic writing consists of symbols depicting physical objects, and in the earliest examples these symbols were carved in stone. When writing on papyrus became widely practised their form was simplified to the 'hieratic' or sacred script, used by the priests, and then further simplified for business or popular use to the 'demotic' or people's script. In this last the pictorial element was entirely lost. At first the symbols were direct drawings of things, but the system became more useful when the same drawings were used not only for the actual objects depicted, but also for things or abstract ideas which had the same sounds as these objects. Thus in reading hieroglyphic writing we must pay attention both to the objects depicted by the symbols and to their sounds.

Plate 42 shows one side of the pyramid-shaped top of a fallen and broken obelisk in Thebes which was 29·5 metres (96½ ft) high and weighed 325 tonnes. Without Champollion we could have admired the splendid composition of the figures, evidently a god extending his hands in blessing over a kneeling king, but would have understood nothing more of the meaning. Now we can read the signs, starting at the upper right column: 'Words spoken by Amon-Re, lord of the heavens: I have given [2nd column] the rule of the Two Lands entirely to my daughter [3rd column; the name is outlined in a *cartouche*] Maat-ka-Re as she desires. May she live!' This Maat-ka-Re, 'righteousness is the essence of (the Sun-god) Re', is known as the only woman Pharaoh of importance, usually known by her maiden name of Hatshepsut, 'pinnacle of noble women', and famed for the magnificent Temple of the Dead which she had built against the steep rock wall guarding the Valley of the Kings (Plate 9). After a reign of twenty years this queen was forcibly deposed *c.* 1480 B.C. by her half-brother and husband, Thothmes III, who had her statues everywhere torn down and her name effaced. The top of our obelisk happily survived this destruction, but was, however, the victim of another. On the photo one can plainly see that the figure of the god Amon with his tall feathers lies deeper in the stone than that of the queen, depicted as a man; the same is true of the hieroglyphs in the right-hand column giving his name and title, 'lord of heaven'. In roughly 1377 B.C. Amenophis IV came to the throne. He wished the solar disk, Aton, to be the only god venerated. His fanaticism drove him to have the name of the supreme god Amon everywhere effaced. The zealous servants of Akhenaton ('it is pleasing to Aton'), as he called himself, even climbed the tall obelisk of Hatshepsut to cut away Amon's name and title. This religious reformer, who had built a brand-new capital exactly between Memphis and Thebes, near the modern el-Amarna, died *c.* 1358 B.C. misunderstood by his people and leaving the state in chaos. Then the priests of Amon set about rectifying the wrong done to their god and restored his name and images as well as they could, as we see here on our obelisk. The traces of the restoration, however, have remained visible. From this example one sees that now, thanks to the work of Champollion and his successors, the dead stones of Egypt speak to us.

Eloquent, too, are numerous papyri, covered with writing, which survived in this rainless land. At the very beginning of their history, around 3000 B.C., the Egyptians evolved a method of making writing material from the papyrus reeds which grew in the Nile Delta. Long strips of reed were laid side by side to the required width, and another layer of shorter strips was placed across them at right angles. These two layers were then soaked in water, pressed, and left to dry in the sun. The resulting sheets were joined together into a long roll on which marks could be traced with the aid of ink and thin styluses. These signs were also hieroglyphs, but in the cursive form which is called hieratic script.

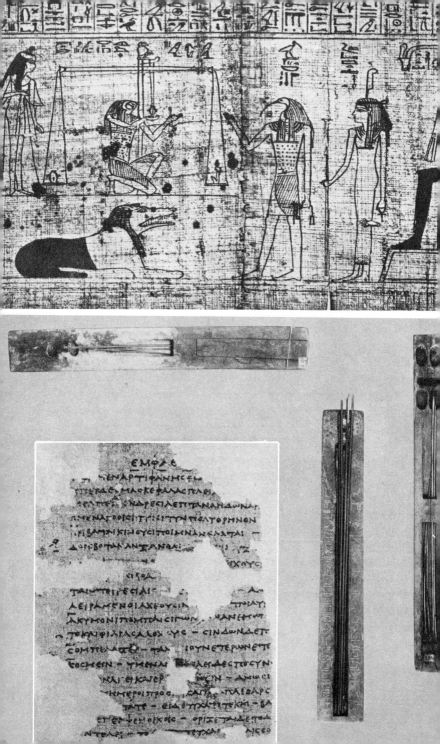

Sometimes drawings were added, often in colour and as carefully drawn as the best medieval miniatures. Many such drawings are found in the collection of texts which, after 1600 B.C., used to be buried with embalmed dead and which is usually known as the *Book of the Dead*. Our photograph (Plate 43) of a vignette from the copy in the Museum voor Oudheden in Leiden (which also possesses the writers' palettes shown in Plate 44) shows Osiris, the god of the dead, in his chapel. Before him stands Maat, goddess of justice, and in front of her the god Thoth, who supervises Horus' manipulation of the scales. Upon these scales the heart of the dead person, in this case a woman who looks on in suspense, is being weighed against justice, in the form of a miniature statue of Maat. Under the scales lies a monster of hell. Besides all sorts of magic formulae the *Book of the Dead* also contains speeches like the following, which the deceased had to pronounce before his heavenly judge: 'I have done no wrong, I have not robbed, I have not been covetous, I have not stolen, I have killed no man, I have not given short measure of corn . . .' And more positive: 'I have done what is pleasing to the gods, I have given bread to the hungry and water to the thirsty and clothes to the naked and a passage to those with no boat . . .'

In Mesopotamia there were no papyrus plants. In ancient times the southern part was one of the most fertile regions in the world, since the soil was composed entirely of thick river clay. In the fourth millennium before Christ the Sumerians had already discovered that a mark scratched on a flattened lump of clay was ineffaceable once the clay had hardened in the sun, and also that drawings could serve to depict ideas and messages. Soon they began to stylize their drawings of all sorts of objects. The stylus left a thicker impression where it was first pressed on the clay, making the signs wedge-shaped (Lat. *cuneus*, 'wedge', hence the term cuneiform writing). This stylization soon made the original object unrecognizable, while other signs were added in order to

Plate 43. Vignette from the Leiden *Book of the Dead*.

Plate 44. Papyrus with a classical work from the third century B.C. Surrounding it, palettes of Egyptian scribes.

express more elements of the language unambiguously. When the country of the Sumerians was occupied by the Accadians, c. 2250 B.C., the latter used the cuneiform writing for their own Semitic language. Many signs were given different meanings and sound values, and new signs were added. This process continued throughout the turbulent history of Mesopotamia, and in the meantime cuneiform writing came to be used outside this region. In a study of the evolution of cuneiform writing which appeared in 1926 35,438 different signs were recorded.

Happily for us, the Elamites, who lived in the mountainous country north of ancient Sumer, also adopted the system and greatly simplified it, leaving only 113 syllabic signs. The Persians further reduced these to 41. The enthralling history of the decipherment of this language begins indeed with texts which travellers had copied in Persepolis, the 'City of the Persians'. There were found inscriptions which, as later appeared, rendered the same text in three different languages, Persian, Elamite, and Babylonian. In 1802 the German teacher Grotefend very keenly observed that in what was apparently the simplest section occurred the names of the Persian kings Hystaspes, Darius, and Xerxes; this gave him the equivalent of thirteen letters. An English Indian army officer, Rawlinson, very interested in the deciphering work, succeeded after superhuman efforts in making a copy of the enormous inscription which Darius (522–486) had had carved on the steep rock-face of Bisutun (Behistun). There, 120 metres (390 ft) above the ground, stood a lengthy text, in the three above-mentioned languages and scripts. The deciphering of the third, which contained the largest number of different signs, was made easier by the collaboration of many scholars and by the influx of reliefs from the Assyrian towns being excavated at this time, in which the meaning of the inscriptions was often made clear by the pictures. In 1848 the Royal Asiatic Society gave a

Plate 45. Statue of a scribe of the Old Kingdom, from the Museum voor Oudheden in Leiden. He holds an unrolled papyrus on his knee and writes with his left hand. The sculptor did not devote much attention to the body; the head, on the other hand, is lovingly carved, 'a completely human portrait with delicate, well-formed features, pleasing both in full face and in profile'.

text to four experts – Rawlinson, Talbot, an Irish priest, and a German – and asked them to translate it independently of each other. The four results were identical in all essential points, and the gateway to Mesopotamian antiquity was open at last. Since this time scholars have assiduously studied the refinements of the Babylonic-Assyrian language in every phase of its development, and with the knowledge obtained have conquered other domains, that of the Sumerian language and culture, for example, and the completely forgotten world of the Hittites in Asia Minor.

In this limited space it has only been possible to show a few specimens of the very considerable number of cuneiform documents: the Legal Code of King Hammurabi of Babylon (*c*. 1728–1686; Plates 46–7), engraved upon stone, and a few texts on clay (Plate 48). The deciphering of a great number of documents has made it possible to establish a chronology and thus to reconstruct ancient history. In this the lists of kings found in several towns of Mesopotamia have proved of immeasurable value. These lists gave the names of a number of successive rulers of a city or state with the length of their reign. Important events were dated according to the year of the ruler's reign, and also eclipses of the sun and moon. A number of definite facts could thus be determined with the help of modern astronomy. There were also texts

Plate 46. Top of the pillar of black diorite, 2 metres (6½ ft) high, on which King Hammurabi engraved a code of laws *c*. 1690 B.C. It contains 282 paragraphs as well as an introduction and a conclusion. Carried away from Babylon by the Elamites as a trophy, it was found in 1902 at Susa. Left, the King, standing and respectfully carrying his right hand to his mouth; right, the sun god Shamash, who sits on a throne representing a temple; his feet rest on a stool which symbolizes a mountain range; the four pairs of horns on his head indicate his divinity. As protector of the law, Shamash hands the King a staff and a ring.

Plate 47. As a specimen of the cuneiform text the beginning of paragraph 25 is shown here. Each sign has the value of a syllable. Beginning at the top right the eight columns read: *shum-ma i-na bît a-wi-lim/i-sha-tum/in-na-pi-ikh-ma/a-wi-lum/sha a-na bu-ul-li-im/il-li-ku/a-na nu-ma-at/be-el bîtim*, which means 'if in a man's house/a fire/has broken out/and if some person/who in order to put it out/has gone there/on the property/of the master of the house …', and Hammurabi continues '… has cast his eyes and has taken the property of the master of the house, that man shall be cast into this same fire'.

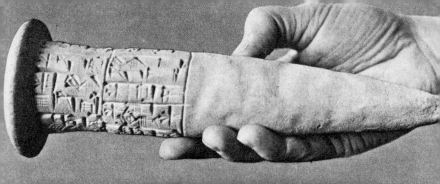

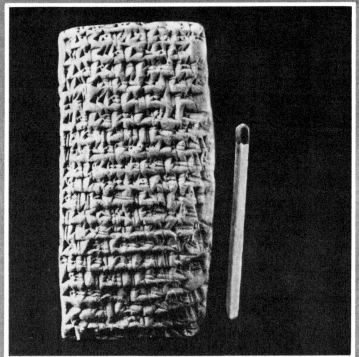

referring to campaigns against and treaties with other countries in which kings mentioned the names of their foreign colleagues.

There is unfortunately no space to give a large table of ancient eastern history similar to Figure 5 (pp. 164–5). It would have to begin with the year 3000 B.C. and give on the left the history of Egypt in its four periods: the Old Kingdom (2850–2050), the Middle Kingdom (2050–1780), the New Kingdom (1610–715), and the Later Period (715–332), while the right-hand side would show the principal dynasties and kingdoms of Mesopotamia. In the centre, roughly between 1650 and 1200 B.C., would stand the mighty kingdom of the Hittites, and beside it, between 1460 and 1300, the buffer state of Mitanni in the Khâbûr region. It would then be obvious at a glance that Israel as a state, i.e. under David, only entered the scene comparatively late, c. 1000 B.C. This fact is extremely important, for the decipherment has revealed to us not

Plate 48. *Top*: a clay 'nail', probably used as a wall decoration in the temples of south Mesopotamia. This specimen, from the De Liagre Böhl collection in Leiden, comes from Lagash. The text informs us that the ruler of this city, Entemena (c. 2350 B.C.), has built a house for his gods and has designed the interior, and further that he has signed a pact of friendship with the ruler of Uruk (the Biblical Erech). *Centre*: letter from a Babylonian officer (the match serves to indicate the scale!), dating from the years before the destruction of the empire in 538. Mention is made of a certain Gubarru (Greek Gobryas), probably the person who played a part in the fall of Babylon. One also reads the names *nabu-kudurri-usur*, 'Nebo protect the landmark', spelled in the Bible Nebuchadnezzar (in some versions Nabuchodonosor), and *Nergal-shar-usur*, 'Nergal protect the King', who is mentioned in the Bible as a commander of Nebuchadnezzar at the conquest of Jerusalem in 587 B.C. under the name Nergal-sharezer (Jer 39.3), and who later, in 559, became king of Babylon. *Foot*: contracts concerning deliveries of corn, also from the De Liagre Böhl collection in Leiden; left, one of these contracts in its 'envelope'. The specimen on the right, being held beside the envelope, is dated in the 44th year of King Shulgi of Ur, c. 2000 B.C. Clay offered an indestructibility that modern paper cannot provide. When the small contract had been written and the names of the witnesses added before the clay was dry, it was enclosed in a layer of wet clay, the 'envelope', on to which the text was thus transferred, together with the names of the witnesses. The seals of the contractors were then affixed. If, after the signing of the contract, one of them maintained that alterations had been made to the text, the judge had the envelope broken open and the original text appeared.

only the history but also the culture of the nations before Israel, in many of its religious and social expressions.

In a good bookshop anyone can now buy large works containing translations of ancient eastern texts which in one way or another are of importance for the study of the Old Testament. Besides historical texts one finds accounts of the Creation and prehistorical events, all sorts of epics and myths, prayers, and songs of praise, love songs, proverbs full of worldly wisdom, philosophical works, prophecies and oracles, liturgical instructions, legal codes of every kind, letters, and so on, all translated from the languages which were used in Egypt, Mesopotamia, Syria, Palestine, and the land adjoining. A first acquaintance with these texts causes many to exclaim 'These people feel and speak as they do in the Bible!' A closer examination of these mainly pre-Israelite texts leads one to say that Israel was indeed completely a product of its environment. And yet Israel possessed a quality inalienably its own, a quality which was never so obvious as in our day, thanks to the revelation of the Eastern past.

Plate 49. In ancient Mesopotamia everyone of importance had his own seal, a small cylinder made of precious or semi-precious stone with a picture, usually religious, engraved on it and sometimes also a text. A hole was bored through it lengthways so that it could be worn on a chain round the neck. The owner rolled it across the wet clay of a written tablet by way of a signature. On the envelope at the foot of Plate 48 two such imprints are visible, one at the top and one at the bottom. We show here a few specimens from the tens of thousands which are known to exist. They are the object of a special branch of archaeological study. *Top*: the sun god rising between the mountains. *In the third row*: two impressions from seals showing scenes from mythology: to the left is a ziggurat, to the right two people near the tree of life, with the serpent. *Foot*: a seal of precious green stone with rings of shell and a silver knob; to judge by the picture it probably belonged to a priest in charge of a temple herd. *The second seal from the top* was found at Beth-shan and is characteristic of seals used in Palestine: one sees here Egyptian influences (including the so-called sign of life), combined with motifs from north Mesopotamia.

Plate 50. Much cultural and historical information is derived from the discovery of numerous 'stelae', slabs of stone erected in honour of divinities or in commemoration, decorated in bas-relief and inscribed with texts. We give here three specimens. *Left*: a stele 1·35 metres (4½ ft) high, from the time of Tiglath-pileser III, found at *Arslân-Tash* west of Haran; the storm god Hadad stands on a young bull in a warlike attitude with a thunder bolt in each hand and a star symbol on his head. *Upper right*: a stele of black basalt, 1·83 metres (6 ft) high, found in the land of Moab, south of the Arnon near *el-Baluʿa*, probably of the twelfth or eleventh century B.C. Between two gods in Egyptian dress stands a man praying, probably the King of Moab. The inscription on the top is scarcely visible and has not yet been deciphered. Equally indicative of strong Egyptian influence in Canaan is the small limestone stele (*below right*), 28 cm (11 in.) high, dating from the fourteenth century B.C. and found in Beth-shan. Upper left can be seen the enthroned Mekal, the local baal of this city.

The Technique of Biblical Geography

Early one morning in March 1928 a Syrian farmer was ploughing his strip of land near the Mediterranean Sea, close to the chalky and sometimes steep wall of a bay which his fellow-countrymen called *Minet el-Beida*, 'the white harbour'. Suddenly his primitive plough struck a heavy stone. When he had finally succeeded in lifting it he saw that it was the key-stone of a vault; the space beneath was a burial chamber full of inviting objects. It was then that the man did something for which archaeologists and Biblical scholars will always be grateful. He resisted the temptation to sell the dishes and jewellery for a good price in the antique market and reported his find to the authorities, at that time French. Archaeologists examined the tomb and its surroundings and then devoted their attention to the extensive tell lying half a mile inland. This was called *Râs Shamra*, 'hill of fennel', apparently because it was covered with this plant. A trial trench proved promising and it was decided to excavate. In the very first campaign, in 1929, on the highest part of the hill, spectacular finds were made, including a temple and a library containing numerous clay tablets covered with an unfamiliar kind of cuneiform writing. An old Phoenician trading city, of which Minet el-Beida had apparently been the harbour, thus lay farther north than had ever been supposed. The scholars racked their brains to discover the name of this city. Could this be Zemar, already mentioned in Egyptian texts from the time of Thothmes III as a strong coastal city of Canaan and whose inhabitants, the Zemarites, are mentioned in the Bible after those of the island city of Arvad (Gn 10.18)? During the first campaign a stele (an upright memorial

stone; cf. Plate 50) was found, dedicated by an Egyptian official to the god Set of Saphon, a common city name also occurring in ancient Palestine as Zaphon (Jos 13.27). Could this have been the name of the city? No, said other scholars; for in the state archives of the Pharaohs Amenophis III and IV, which the latter had had transferred to his new capital near el-Amarna (see p. 63), and whose correspondence with the rulers of Asia (377 clay tablets or fragments) has cast so much light upon the situation in Canaan *c*. 1400–1370 B.C., an important role is played by Ugarit, a town which certainly lay far to the north. This must be Râs Shamra. These scholars proved to be right. When the new cuneiform writing (an alphabet of 29 letters) had been deciphered in an incredibly short time, the texts showed that the excavated city was indeed identical with Ugarit.

Anyone who studies Biblical geography meets the same sort of problem. On the one hand he has a number of texts at his disposal, beginning with the Bible itself. In the historical books especially many place names occur, usually in the narratives, occasionally in primarily geographical texts like Genesis 10 and above all Joshua 13–21. In addition he has non-Biblical texts, both ancient (for example the lists of conquered regions and cities of Asia which the Pharaohs, beginning with Thothmes III, had carved on the walls of their temples and the bases of their statues (Plate 51) and the accounts of the campaigns of the Assyrian kings, etc.) and more recent (the Graeco-Roman writers, the Biblical-geographical works of Eusebius, Jerome, Arabian, medieval, and later scholars). On the other hand the Biblical geographer has the land before him as it is now, with its towns

Plate 51. Side of the statue of Rameses II at Luxor, visible on the left of Plate 73. Each of the figures in the row underneath, depicted as Semites with their arms bound behind their backs and linked together by a halter around their necks, represents a region or city conquered in 'Asia'. One finds here well-known names such as that of the kingdom of Mitanni (the second figure from the left), which between 1460 and 1300 B.C. formed a buffer state between Assyria (fourth figure), the Hittites, who had penetrated far into Syria (last in the row, not visible), and Egypt. In between are the names of regions and cities which have not yet all been identified. One can easily understand the importance of such lists for the study of the ancient political geography of Canaan.

Plate 52. Ostraca and seals. As writing material for notes and messages the ancient Israelites liked to use potsherds, which were provided in plenty by the household, rather than the expensive papyrus. Here are three examples of such potsherds ('ostraca'). *Below left*: a letter from Samaria, eighth century B.C., unfortunately broken off at the left-hand side. Two of the lines scratched upon it begin with the name Baruch, the third with the name Imna, which also occurs in the Bible. *Below right*: one of the famous letters from Lachish. In 1953, in the gate building of the city, were found a number of potsherds, of which unhappily only eighteen still bore traces of lines written in ink in a flowing hand. Six of these presented a legible and coherent text. These letters were written to Yaôsh, apparently the Jewish governor of the district of Lachish in the anxious years of the Babylonian menace between 597 and 587. The writers, apparently officers serving in this area, employ exactly the same style as Baruch, the friend and secretary of Jeremiah, whom they undoubtedly all knew, if only by hearsay. Almost all the names of Judaeans mentioned in these letters occur also in the Bible. Our photograph shows the reverse of letter 3, giving the last five lines of what a certain Hoshaiah (cf. Jer 42.1) writes to Yaôsh and in which he mentions a letter from the royal official Tobiah addressed to Sallum, son of Jaddua, in the name of the prophet who says 'Take heed.'

Facing page: top right: an ostracon of the eighth century found in the *Tell el-Qasîleh* slightly NE of Tel-Aviv, the site of a fortified Israelite trading city (it is not yet known which) during the time of the Kings. The line reads 'Ophir gold [cf. Is 13.12] for Beth-horon . . .' Something else probably followed here. The letter and the three lines underneath mean 'thirty shekels'. Beth-horon, i.e. 'the house (temple) of the god Horon', is either the famous double city on the

frontier between Israel and Judah or else a temple in the trading city mentioned. *Top left*: five examples of seals from ancient Israel. They were usually made after the Egyptian model, in the shape of a scarab. This species of beetle lays its eggs in balls made from human or animal dung, which provides food for the larvae. From earliest times this insect was considered in Egypt as the symbol of the sun god who rolls across the sky the luminous ball from which all life emerges. The flat bottoms of the many scarab-shaped seals found in Egypt are decorated with all kinds of figures, formulae, and names. The upper two of our five illustrations show the surface and the impression of an Israelite scarab from Lachish; beneath the figure of a winged beetle stands the name of the owner, Ahimelech. Of the three illustrations beneath, the one on the left shows the impression from a scarab-like seal from Mizpah: above the fighting-cock is the name of the owner, 'Jaazaniah, the servant of the King' (see 2 K 25.23). On the central impression the name Chaman can be read between the feet of a crowned sphinx (with the sign of life in front); below is a locust. Right: the bottom of a seal from the Transjordan; the cuneiform writing runs: 'Adoni-ner, servant of Amminadab' (King of the Ammonites *c*. 650 B.C.).

Foot: four photographs of a rare scarab from the author's collection. It was found in Palestine and probably dates from the sixteenth century B.C. The figure stands in the attitude of a Pharaoh holding his enemies by the hair and on the point of striking. He is, however, obviously a Palestinian and what he is about to strike is Uraeus the serpent, on which he has also set his foot. This serpent is the symbol of Egyptian royal power. The various signs have not yet been fully explained.

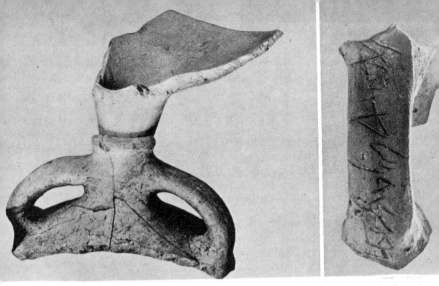

Plates 53–4. Finds from Gibeon. 53: the upper part of a wine jar with the funnel piece; the handles bear names. 54: one of the many handles on which the name Gibeon occurs.

and villages and innumerable ruins and tells, whether he lives there (which is preferable) or possesses very good maps of the region. His problem is to identify the towns named in the Bible and to place them, as far as he can, in the correct locality. This is not always an easy task. If a place mentioned in the Bible is still inhabited under the same name, like Jerusalem, Bethlehem, Heshbon, etc., its identification presents no problem, nor is there any difficulty when the name of the old city is still clearly recognizable in that of its tell or of a place in the immediate neighbourhood, whether inhabited or not. *Tell Ta'annak* cannot be anything but the tell of the Biblical Taanach, near which Barak gave battle (Jg 5.19). The enormous *Tell el-Hosn* must contain the ruins of Biblical Beth-shan, for until 1949 the village of *Beisân*, an Arabic version of the old name, lay close by.

But where the old names have been forgotten and long since replaced by new ones, or where they have been so drastically corrupted as to be unrecognizable in the modern Arabic name for the tell or village, then the archaeologist and geographer must look elsewhere for evidence of identification. In earlier Biblical atlases one finds the town of Lachish indicated on the site of *Tell el-Hesy* (cf. p. 51); *Tell ed-Duweir*, 'the tell of the small monastery', 12 km ($7\frac{1}{2}$ miles) farther east, appeared, however, to correspond more with the literary data. The excavations there (1933–7), in which the famous potsherds covered with writing were found (shown on the left in Plate 52), made identification with Lachish almost certain. Later atlases now reserve *Tell el-Hesy* for the Biblical Eglon, but with a large query. Here is yet another example. According to the ancient texts the Philistine town of Ekron must have stood where the coastal plain merges into the hill country, roughly parallel with Jerusalem. There, indeed, roughly 15 km (9 miles) from the coast, one finds a village called '*Aqir*, apparently a derivation of Ekr(on). Many atlases thus situated the Biblical city there, but tentatively, for no shards of the Biblical period had been found either in or near the village. Israelite scholars have recently investigated the ruin *el-Muqanna'*, about $7\frac{1}{2}$ km ($4\frac{1}{2}$ miles) farther south, and made its identification with Ekron extremely probable. This ruin, however, was considered by many to be the remains of the Biblical Eltekeh, for which another site must now be sought. Biblical Gibeon was usually seen in the village of *el-Jîb*, $9\frac{1}{2}$ km (6 miles) north-west of old Jerusalem (Plate 83). Serious objections were, however, raised against this identification, disputing both the identity of the names and the conformity with the literary data. In the summer of 1956 the American, Pritchard, began a small excavation on this spot. He discovered an enormous round well, 11 metres (36 ft) in diameter, hewn out of the rock, with steps running down the side (Plate 84). This must have been the pool of Gibeon (2 S 2.13). The soil with which it was filled contained a large number of shards and wine jar handles and even funnels, and on 27 of the jar handles was the name Gibeon (Plates 53–4). For the first time in sixty-six years of excavation a Palestinian ruin provided its own visiting-cards!

The Chronicles of the Old Testament

Until late into the Middle Ages Jews and Christians were of the opinion that the first five books of the Bible were written by Moses himself. This great work, known as 'the Law' or, following an old Greek expression, 'the Pentateuch' (the work 'composed of five scrolls'), was inseparably linked with the founder of Israel's religion. It dealt precisely with events from the creation of the world up to and including the mighty happenings on which the religion of Israel throughout the centuries that followed was to be based: the journey out of Egypt to freedom, the Covenant on Mount Sinai, and the journey to the Promised Land. Here Moses himself had played the leading role, and all that he recorded concerning former times he could know by tradition. Could he not trace his descent back to Adam? It was even assumed that this greatest of all prophets, having learned the facts concerning the creation (Gn 1), had completed the work with the story of his own end (Dt 34.1–8). Only in the Renaissance did men begin to doubt the truth of this age-old tradition. This was not so much because people at this time were distrustful of any kind of tradition. The Pentateuch, like other old writings, had now begun to be read in the original Hebrew. This was rendered possible for many by the distribution of printed Bibles in Hebrew, and now more attention was paid than in previous centuries to the literary qualities of this work.

It was soon discovered that the 'Law of Moses' contained many differences in style, repetitions, and contradictions which seemed to make the hypothesis of one author unlikely. Some also argued that at the time of Moses writing had either not been discovered or was still so primitive that such a varied and, in some parts, highly skilled literary work could not possibly have been written. That this last argument no longer holds water needs no further demonstration after the exposition on pp. 61–73. As a reminder Plate 45 shows the charming statuette of an Egyptian writer who lived 1000 years before Moses and who could afford this immortalization thanks to the career he had made for himself after a lengthy schooling and the zealous study of a literature which by this time was already regarded as classical.

If Moses was really trained for a high office at the Pharaoh's court in the eastern Delta around 1300 B.C. he was probably familiar, not only with the Egyptian writing, but also with the cuneiform script used for diplomatic correspondence with Asia. This means that, technically speaking, he was quite capable of writing an extensive work like the Pentateuch. In actual fact, however, this work was written centuries after his death. It is generally assumed that the text as we know it only came into existence in the 5th century B.C. At this period learned priests –

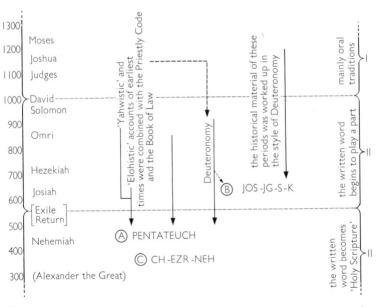

Figure 4

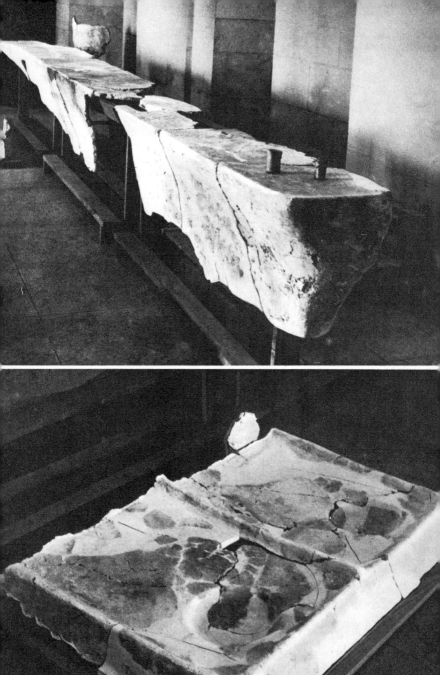

after the Exile it was they who led the people – collected all kinds of story series and compilations of laws dating from former centuries and amplified them with material conserved in their own circles. All this they transformed into one whole in the manner which seemed to them best for the Jewish community. This process is indicated in Figure 4: oral traditions from the 'Hebrew' period I, laid down in various collections during the 'Israelite' period II, were expanded into the Pentateuch (A) of our Bible during the 'Jewish' period III. One should also note the position of the two other great historical works. The books of Joshua, Judges, Samuel, and Kings, considered by many to have formed originally one whole (B), were written under Josiah (see p. 114) and revised during the Exile. Chronicles, together with Ezra and Nehemiah (C), was written by a Levite in the fourth century B.C. Just as with (A), the authors of (B) and (C) employed all kinds of traditional material of differing type and origin; they too were strongly guided in the compilation of their books by the spiritual needs of their contemporaries and by their vision of the past. From this it follows that the more or less literal retelling of the content of (A), (B), and (C) may not be presented without further

Plate 55. Remains of a long table found in the large writing room in *Qumrân*, now in the Rockefeller Museum in Jerusalem.

Plate 56. Part of another writing table. The hollows contained water in which it was probably customary to dip the fingers before writing the sacred name of Israel's god. The four consonants of this name, *Yhwh* (vowels were not written at this time), were represented in *Qumrân* either by the customary Hebrew letters, or the then old-fashioned script of before the Exile (like that of the Lachish letters; see the left of Plate 52), or else with four dots. In later centuries, when reciting Biblical texts, the Jews were accustomed to replace the Name-of-four-letters (tetragram) by *Adonai*, which means 'the Lord'. When vowels were added to the sacred texts, the vowels of the word *Adonai* (a mute *e*, an *o*, and an *a*), which was to be pronounced, were added to the four sacred consonants. In the Middle Ages this fact was no longer understood and thus the four letters *Yhwh* were read with the vowels of *Adonai*, giving rise to the completely meaningless form of *Jehovah*. It is not entirely certain how the original sacred tetragram was pronounced. On good grounds scholars write and pronounce 'Yahweh' unless the name is avoided and replaced by 'the Lord' or 'the Eternal'.

comment as 'history'. This word is nowadays reserved for a summing-up of past events based upon a critical investigation of the sources. Anyone compiling a history of Israel must first investigate every statement in the three works to decide in which environment it originated, how much it has altered in the course of being handed down, and why the ultimate adapter incorporated it into his book in just this form and in this place. These questions must definitely be asked, for many continue to cling unconsciously to the idea of the Biblical historian who, sitting concealed with his legs crossed and a scroll in his lap, notes down without error all that he sees and hears. Critical examination of the texts – corroborated but not supplanted by archaeological discoveries – is necessary despite suggestions in certain popular

Plate 57. *Top*: one of the first and most famous finds at *Qumrân*. This scroll, 26 cm (10¼ in.) wide and 7·34 metres (24 ft) long when unrolled, was found in a tall jar in cave No. 1 (see Plate 161). It contains the entire book of Isaiah as it is found in our Bible. On the second line of the completely visible column, after a white patch, begins Isaiah Chapter 40: 'A voice cries: "In the wilderness prepare the way of the Lord" . . .', which words, slightly altered, are applied in the New Testament to John the Baptist, the voice in the wilderness. *Centre*: a particularly large fragment, 23 cm (9 in.) long and 11 cm (4 in.) broad, found in cave No. 4. It is part of a scroll which contained a commentary on Isaiah. The intact column reads: 'The meaning of the word concerns the end of time, at the destruction [?] of the earth by the sword and by famine; and it shall be in the time of the visitation of the earth: Woe to those who rise early in the morning that they may run after strong drink . . .' (Is 5.11–14). Then follows the commentary: 'These are the men of scorn who dwell in Jerusalem. They who have rejected the law of the Lord of Hosts, and have despised the words of the Holy One of Israel . . .' (Is 5.24–5). After this follows again: 'This is the community of the men of scorn who are in Jerusalem . . .' One sees how the members of the Dead Sea sect considered their own situation and the circles of their enemies in Jerusalem to have been already described in the old prophetic texts. *Foot*: another fragment, seven-eighths of its true size, in which words of Is 54.11–12 are applied to the community of the elect (cf. Revelation 21). *Right*: reproduction in actual size of a phylactery or amulette. In Mt 23.5 this is what is meant by the 'phylacteries' of the Pharisees. This specimen dates from the time of Christ and was found in a cave on the *Wâdi Muraba'at*, 20 km (12½ miles) south of *Qumrân*. Three of the prescribed texts are written on this strip in extremely small letters, Ex 13.1–10, 13.11–16, and Dt 11.13–21. It was found in a small bag folded together with a smaller fragment on which is written the equally prescribed text of Dt 6.4–9: 'Hear O Israel . . .' (known as the *Shema*).

87

books. Such examination often leads to hypotheses where one would prefer certainties, especially so far as period I of our plan is concerned. Here hypothesis must be preferred to false certainty, out of respect for the Bible.

But are not the *Qumrân* texts of any help? No, the sect established here (for more detail, see pp. 199–211) already knew the three records as canonized holy scripture. In the sacred atmosphere of their writing room, seated at long tables (Plate 55), they carefully copied the holy books, dipping their fingers into the water-filled cavities whenever they wrote the most holy name of God (Plate 56). Their Biblical scrolls (Plate 57) are extremely important for the study of the Biblical books which had achieved a definitive form long before their time; but they do not tell us how these books came to be recorded.

The Patriarchs

As no other nation of antiquity Israel preserved and cherished the memories of its origin. In the time of the Judges the tribes were already accustomed, during the offering of the first fruits in Yahweh's sanctuary, to profess their origin in these words: 'A wandering Aramaean was my father; and he went down into Egypt . . . and there he became a nation, great, mighty, and populous. And the Egyptian treated us harshly, and afflicted us and laid upon us hard bondage. Then we cried to the Lord the God of our fathers, and the Lord heard our voice . . . and the Lord brought us out of Egypt with a mighty hand . . . and He brought us unto this place and gave us this land . . . and behold, now I bring the first of the fruit of the ground which Thou, O Lord, hast given me'. From the use of the personal pronoun one sees how strongly the Israelite felt himself one with his fore-fathers. It is also clear that even this early profession of faith (handed down in Dt 26.5–10) already contains the elements of the great themes which dominate the Pentateuch: the wandering fathers of the tribes who founded a nation in Egypt; the slavery and deliverance; the leading of the people to the Promised Land (only the theme of Mount Sinai and the Covenant is missing here). The first theme is developed in the familiar stories of Genesis 12–50 concerning the adventures of Abraham and Sarah, their son Isaac, and the latter's twin sons Esau and Jacob, of whom the last named, after Joseph's marvellous career, settles in Egypt with all his family.

These stories, which are linked together by the recurring theme of God's promises and His personal guidance of the main

characters, appear, on analysis, to be an extraordinary amalgamation of differing elements of various dates, ranging from popular elements to stories with a profound theological import. According to the Hebrew conception the patriarch lived on in his tribe in a very real sense. For this reason, writers liked to explain a characteristic or experience of the tribe by telling a story about the patriarch, often laying particular stress on the meaning of his name. For instance, at one time, the 'sons of Jacob' formed a tribal unity; and (in the time of David) they conquered the Edomites, who lived in the mountain country of Seir. These facts were amalgamated as follows: the word *edom* means 'red', and *seir* has something to do with 'hairy'. The name Jacob, originally perhaps 'may he (God) protect', was associated by the Israelites with the word *akeb*, 'heel'; a verb, probably derived from this word, has in the third person the form *jacob*, 'he lays snares for the heel, he is artful, he deceives'. The story of the twins, of whom the elder, Esau (the ancestor of the Edomites), is 'red' and 'hairy' and whom Jacob seizes by the heel, afterwards to 'deceive' and dominate him (Gn 25.22–6), is thus really a piece of folk etymology. The historical event in David's reign is here combined with a much older tradition, that the Edomites were of the same ethnic group as the Israelites, that they were 'twin brothers'. In the same way Israel was conscious of kinship with the trans-Jordan peoples of Moab and Ammon (whom they nevertheless hated). Their names resembled the Hebrew words for 'father' and 'fatherly', hence the not very edifying story of their common origin from Lot, a nephew of Abraham (Gn 19.30–38).

Plate 58. The region around the city of *Harrân* has been under investigation since 1951. Our plate shows *Sultantepe*, 25 km (15½ miles) north of Harrân. This tell has yielded, among other things, many hundreds of clay tablets from an Assyrian library.

Plate 59. Reconstruction sketch of the ziggurat of Ur, whose ground surface covers 62·5 metres by 43 metres (205 by 140 ft).

Plate 60. One of the sides of this massive structure; the man indicates the scale.

Plate 61. Nomads in the desert east of Palestine near a pool recently created by the Jordan government.

During the Assyrian crisis, the great Isaiah was to characterize the attitude of God's people as faith; later, during and after the Exile, the already centuries-old practice of circumcision obtained its full significance as a symbol of the Covenant. For this reason the attitude of Abraham, prototype of the nation which he bore 'in his loins', is described as faith (Gn 15.6), and circumcision obtained an essential place in the covenant of God with him (Gn 17).

These are but a few examples, sufficient, it is hoped, to make it clear that the varied whole of Genesis 12–50 should not be considered merely as the simple account of the experiences of a few

Plate 62. A Bedouin camp in the broad valley of the Brook Zered which divided the former regions of Moab and Edom.

Plate 63. The Jabbok, looking east.

individuals who lived in antiquity. These chapters are much richer in meaning. Israel's peculiar historical consciousness was closely bound up with its conviction that it was still the object of God's personal interest, an interest which he had begun to show to the patriarchs. It is precisely for this reason that the memory of the patriarchs remained alive, changing and developing through the ages so that it is now impossible to disentangle those details which most interest us today: what the tribal fathers were like as individuals, what their family relationship was to each other, and what exactly happened to each of them. We are obliged to be content with a few main lines, which, however, fit extremely well into the picture we now possess of the situation in the east towards the middle of the second millennium B.C.

Originating from Ur, Abraham's family settled near Haran (Plate 58). The names of several cities in that region appear in the genealogy of Abraham: cf. Haran, Nahor, Til-taruhi, Sarugi, and

Plate 64. View of *Tell Deir 'Alla* in the Jordan valley near the Jabbok, probably the Biblical Succoth, looking west. Behind the tell, the bed of the Jordan; behind that, the central mountain country.

Plate 65. Aerial photograph of the plain in front of Shechem, taken from the north: 1 = Mount Gerizim; 2 = the massif of Mount Ebal; 3 = tell of ancient Shechem, to the left the small village of *Balâta*; 4 = unfinished church above Jacob's Well; 5 = the point from which Plate 67 was taken; 6 = the road to the south, to Bethel and Jerusalem; 7 = the road to the north, to Tirzah, Tibhath, Beth-shan, etc.; 8 = the road to Samaria and the coastal plain; 9 = the road to the Jordan valley.

Plate 66 (*following page*). Aerial photograph, taken almost vertically, of the mountain pass between Mount Ebal and Mount Gerizim, which can be seen left and right below. Between the small village of *Balâta* and the refugee camp, top right, one can see a white building in a garden; this is the unfinished church above Jacob's Well. On the left can be seen the tell with the traces of the German excavations undertaken in 1913–14 and continued from 1926 to 1934. Since 1956 (the photograph dates from 1953) an American expedition has been digging here every year.

Plate 67 (*following page*). A view through the pass from the east, from a point below 5 on Plate 65. Mount Gerizim, left, with the refugee camp in front of it, is completely visible; Mount Ebal, to the right, partly so.

Plate 68. An ancient oak near Hebron.

Phaliga, and Haran and Nahor, 'brothers' of Abraham, and Terah, Serug, and Peleg, his 'ancestors' (Gn 11.18–26). A group of the clan, Abraham and Lot, the 'father' of Moab and Ammon, journeyed southwards from here to Canaan, without, however, abandoning all contact with those who had remained behind in Aram-naharaim, or Paddan-aram as the region around Haran was also called. They lived as pastoral nomads and travelled with their sheep, goats, and donkeys from one watering-place to another (cf. Plate 61). They liked to pitch their tents (cf. Plate 62) in the country between the waterless plains and the densely populated

Plates 69–71. Rock formations on the shores of the Dead Sea. The projection in Plate 70, 15 metres (50 ft) high, resembles a fleeing woman and is called 'Lot's wife' by the Arabian inhabitants of this region, who also usually call the Dead Sea *Bahr Lût*, the 'sea of Lot'. 71: this figure in the distance, from a boat.

regions of the towns. One of their routes lay through the valley of the Jabbok (Plate 63; note the two nomad tents) where Penuel (also spelled Peniel) lay, into the valley of the Jordan, past Succoth, now a striking tell (Plate 64), across the river to the plain in front of Shechem, in the heart of the country (Plates 65–7, described on p. 37). Across the central mountain ridge they travelled southwards, past Bethel and Hebron, where age-old traditions concerning the origin of the Dead Sea and the remarkable rock formations (Plates 69–71) were linked with their passage (Gn 18, 19), to wander finally in the Negeb, the land of the south, and from there, driven by hunger, to descend towards the fertile Delta. Around 1890 B.C. the Egyptian ruler Chnumhotep had a group of such Semitic nomads depicted on a wall of his tomb (Plate 72). With their multi-coloured garments, their arms, their waterskins and musical instruments, they give a good picture of what Israel's forefathers must have been like.

Plate 72. A group of 'Asiatics' pay their respects to the Egyptian district governor Chnumhotep. From a wall painting in his tomb at *Beni-hasan*, 270 km (169 miles) south of Cairo. The group of nomads, here cut into three, forms there a continuous whole. Behind the Egyptian official who presents the group to the much larger figure of Chnumhotep and upon whose papyrus one can read, among other things, the date (the 6th year of Sesostris II, i.e. roughly 1892 B.C.), follows another Egyptian. Then comes the leader of the group, who makes a respectful gesture with his right hand. Between the horns of the ibex which he is offering one sees the crook with white stripes (cf. Gn 30.37) which on Egyptian pictures marks a Bedouin ruler. The hieroglyphs in front of his head give his title: 'ruler from a foreign land', those in front of his legs the name *Ibsha* (also read as Abisar). The inscription at the top means 'Arrival of black paint for the eyes, brought to him by 37 Asiatics'. The sign for the word 'Asiatics' is a bound man! The number 37 is unfortunately not visible on our reproduction.

Exodus from the House of Bondage

Of the countless early texts found in Egypt, not one makes any reference to the sojourn of the sons of Jacob in the Delta. One finds no mention of Moses nor of the miraculous escape of the Hebrews across the Red Sea. At the same time, in the Bible narratives, in the books of the patriarchs and in Exodus, the names of the Pharaohs concerned are passed over in silence. This raises the question of where the Bible stories must be located within the framework of the now familiar non-Biblical history.

Roughly along the line now followed by the Suez canal, the Pharaohs of the nineteenth century B.C. built a chain of forts to protect their land against the multitudes of famished nomads from Canaan who were attracted by the fertility of the Delta. They were, however, allowed to enter as traders, as we saw on the painting of chief Ibsha and his family (Plate 72). The former bears above his name a title which means 'ruler of a foreign land'. When, *c.* 1700 B.C., the chain of fortresses proved too weak to repel an invasion of mixed racial groups from Canaan and beyond, who ruled lower Egypt for more than a century, they too were given the same title: *hq'h's.t*, which became in Greek 'Hyksos'. Many scholars believe that the settlement of Jacob's sons in Egypt must be sought in this historical background. Joseph's career would be comprehensible in the court of a Pharaoh who himself originated from Canaan. Around 1570 B.C.

Plate 73. Two statues of Rameses II at Luxor in front of the mighty hall with seven pairs of columns 16 metres (52 ft) high, built by Amenophis III (1413–1377 B.C.) and visible in the centre of Plate 7. The side of the statue on the left is shown in close-up in Plate 51.

the Hyksos were expelled from Thebes in the south, and thus began the great epoch during which the Pharaohs from Amenophis I to Thothmes III expanded their territory northwards as far as the Euphrates. This kingdom collapsed under the rule of the unworldly, religious reformer Amenophis IV who called himself Akhenaton (see p. 63). Horemheb was the name of the general who attempted to put down the revolt which had flared up in Palestine under Akhenaton's weak son-in-law Tutankhamon, and ended by becoming Pharaoh himself (1345–1318). The magnificent reliefs from his tomb near Memphis have found their way to various museums – some of the finest are housed in the Rijksmuseum voor Oudheden in Leiden. In Plate 74 Egyptian officers lead two Palestinian captives in the triumphal procession of Horemheb. Another panel shows a group of Syrians who, as the accompanying text explains, 'not knowing how to remain alive', beg admittance to Egypt, 'according to the custom of your fathers from time immemorial'. After Horemheb the restoration was continued and attained a last peak of power and prosperity under Rameses II (1301–1234).

During the first years of his reign Rameses waged a series of bitter wars against the Hittites who were pressing in from Asia Minor. He concluded a famous peace treaty in 1280. The Egyptian version can still be read on temple walls in Thebes, and the Hittite has been found in Babylonian cuneiform writing upon clay tablets. It is generally thought that the Exodus of the Hebrews under Moses must have taken place during the reign of this Pharaoh. This theory is supported by a number of Palestinian archaeological data, such as traces of destruction and migration of inhabitants which must have occurred in various places at roughly the same time, c. 1200 B.C. In addition, the

Plate 74. Detail from a relief in the funeral chamber which Horemheb had built at Memphis while he was still a general under Akhenaton and Tutankhamon. Of the pieces scattered throughout many museums some are to be found in Leiden, including that showing the prisoners taken by the general in Asia. The detail shows two prisoners, of whom the one on the left has the more pronounced Semitic features. In primitive handcuffs they are dragged along by two Egyptian soldiers, one of whom is hidden by the other.

Plates 75–6. Details from a wall painting at Thebes, showing the making of bricks.

situation in Egypt seems an ideal background for the Biblical data. After the expulsion of the Hyksos rulers, many 'Asiatics' had remained behind in the Delta. They were disliked and mistrusted, and it is understandable that Rameses should have chosen his building labourers from among their ranks. On the well-known scene from the tomb of Rekhmire in Thebes, painted *c*. 1460, one sees a typical 'Asiatic' among the brick-bakers (Plate 75). Under Rameses they undoubtedly formed the majority of those who had to perform this wearying task. These people, who, with other prisoners of war and slaves, formed a distinct social class, were called the '*apiru*. Some scholars connect this term with the word '*ibri*, 'Hebrew', which is indeed employed in the stories of Joseph and the Exodus with striking consistency.

During the increasingly heavy forced labour of his group in the land of Goshen Moses had had his mysterious encounter with God in the majestic surroundings of Mount Sinai, in which he experienced the greatness and solicitude of the 'God of the fathers'. Through narrow passes, through spectacularly coloured rocks (Plate 77), one penetrates into the granite heart of the peninsula to emerge suddenly on to a plateau with a towering range in the background; the left-hand peak, slightly to the rear, is the mountain which centuries of tradition have designated as the mountain of Moses (Plate 78). The caravan in this photograph is en route for a point in the shadowed valley to the left, where the famous monastery of St Catherine lies. It can be seen in Plate 79, taken from the opposite direction, so that the plateau

Plate 77. En route for the heart of the Sinai peninsula.

Plate 78. The mountain mass traditionally thought to be the Biblical Sinai. The round peak on the left-hand side is the *Jebel Músa*, the mountain of Moses, 2,292 metres (7,467 ft) above sea-level, 764 metres (2,506 ft) above the monastery of St Catherine in the valley to the left.

Plate 79. The monastery, developed from a fort which the emperor Justinian founded there in A.D. 530 to safeguard the neighbouring hermits. After flourishing for centuries (sometimes with as many as 400 monks) it decayed. The library contains countless old manuscripts. In 1950 an American expedition made microfilms of about 500,000 pages.

lies in the background. Did Moses lead his group of Hebrews, that 'mixed multitude', which included a considerable 'rabble' (Ex 12.38, Num 11.4), straight to these majestic surroundings after a miraculous crossing of an arm of the Red Sea? Or must we agree with the scholars who hold that the Exodus took place along the northern route? The miraculous crossing would then have taken place on the coast, east of Pelusium (see Figure 7, p. 182), where a mountain of God had also been known from ancient times. The localizations in the Biblical story give no definite confirmation one way or the other (Sea of Reeds, Pi-hahiroth, Migdol, Baal-zephon . . .). Only the provisional finishing point of the journey is certain, the region of springs around Kadesh in south Palestine (it can just be seen on Map 3). Moses and his work have sometimes been compared to a mountain that rises up out of the mist. The outline can be seen only vaguely, but we know that it is there, majestic and imposing.

The Exodus and the Covenant form the basis of Israel's further history. The faith of Israel preserved the nucleus of the facts and extended and enhanced them in daily life, not least in the ever-repeated religious ceremonies. The memory of the exact circumstances grew dim. The historian is compelled to grope in the dark. He is not nearly so certain of the course of events during the Exodus as the film makers of Hollywood, yet much more than they he is conscious of the far-reaching historical effects of this event upon the faith and history of Israel.

Settlement in Canaan

After remaining for many years in the land of Kadesh, in the extreme south of Palestine, Moses went north-eastwards with his Hebrews to the 'plains of Moab' across the Jordan facing Jericho. It is no longer possible to form a complete whole from the scraps of tradition concerning the route followed which are set down in the books of Numbers and Deuteronomy. Moses undoubtedly crossed the deep cleft in the Transjordan highland called in our Bible 'the brook Arnon' (Plate 80). Biblical tradition localizes his leave-taking and death on the top of Mount Nebo (Plate 81, viewed from the south). From the top of this mountain, on which lie the ruins of a church and monastery dating from the sixth century, looking across the Jordan valley, 1,100 metres (3,500 ft) below (right on this photograph), one can indeed survey the whole of the hilly central region of Palestine from Hebron to Galilee including Mount Carmel. Southwards the eye covers a large section of the Dead Sea, and towards the north, in clear weather, one can see as far as the Sea of Galilee and snow-covered Mount Hermon, 180 km (112 miles) from Mount Nebo. The land which throughout all these years Moses had seen in his mind's eye as the ultimate goal of his life's work lay here stretched out before him. But the joy of leading his people into the Promised Land was denied him. This task was reserved for Joshua.

The plan of the Biblical book that bears his name is strikingly simple and its geography (at least so far as the campaigns are concerned) is easy to show on a map (see Map 4). In accordance with the divine command (Ch. 1) Joshua sent men to spy out the

Plate 82. The central hill country viewed from the east from a very great height. In the foreground is the edge of the Jordan valley (the white arrow points to the oval tell of ancient Jericho); behind lies the fantastic desert of Judaea. To the right can be seen the Jordan plain entering the central hill country. Here lay the way from Jericho to Ai and Bethel. In the distance are the white line of dunes and the sea coast, about 60 km (37 miles) from Jericho.

land on the other side of the Jordan (Ch. 2), crossed the Jordan (whose waters divided as did those of the Red Sea) with the twelve tribes (Chs. 3, 4), had the people circumcised and celebrated the Passover (Ch. 5), and then conquered Jericho (Ch. 6). After this, following a natural curve (see Plate 82), he crossed the central mountainous country and took Ai (Chs. 7, 8). He spared Gibeon (Plate 83; see also Plate 84) and its allied cities (Ch. 9), after which he defeated a number of rulers, among them the King of Lachish (Plate 85), and conquered the whole of the south (Ch. 10); then, after the battle by the waters of Merom and the destruction of the important royal city of Hazor (Plates 86–7), he took possession of the northern part of Palestine and thus became master of the whole land (Ch. 12). After this the entire country,

Plate 80. The brook Arnon.

Plate 81. Mount Nebo.

Plate 83. The small village of *el-Jib* on the double hill on which Gibeon stood. The distant peak to the left, marked by a minaret, which rises 150 metres (492 ft) above the plain and is visible for miles around, is probably the 'great high place' where Solomon offered sacrifice (1 K 3.4). Since the fifth century Samuel has been commemorated here, hence the name *Nebi Samwi*, the prophet Samuel.

including the Transjordan which had already been occupied, was divided among the twelve tribes (Chs. 13–22). Joshua then delivered his last exhortations, died, and was buried (Chs. 23, 24).

It is evident that we have here a simplified version of a complicated series of events. This simplification is understandable. The book of Joshua was written under King Josiah (640–609 B.C.), probably as the first section of a larger chronicle (see p. 85), and was revised during the Exile. This work might be considered as a sort of national epic, bearing in mind that in Israel national and religious were one. For Israel's dwelling in Palestine formed an essential part of the creed (see p. 89). Yahweh was not god in general; Yahweh was He who had promised the land of Canaan to the fathers and, faithful to His word, had led their descendants out of Egypt to make of them His own people who would inhabit His land. One can thus appreciate something of the tremendous crisis when the Assyrians conquered the larger part of Palestine in 721. One also senses, however, the revival of national and religious aspirations following the rapid decline of Assyria in the years after 650. Soon Israel would once again inhabit undisturbed

Plate 84. The enormous well in Gibeon; the spiral staircase descends beyond the bottom of the well as far as the spring water.

Plate 85. The city of Lachish according to a sketch made by the excavators.

the entire land of Yahweh. At this period all the earlier traditions still living were assembled in a sort of epic, not solely out of love for the past but also as an expression of revived faith, as well as a stimulus and guiding principle for the national restoration. This is why we are given at the outset a simple and eloquent picture of Israel's entry into the Promised Land. Aided by Yahweh's mighty arm, Joshua entered this land at the head of the twelve tribes. He conquered the entire land, and each tribe was allotted its portion. 'Not one of all the good promises which the Lord had made to the house of Israel had failed; all came to pass' (Jos. 21.45). 'But just as all the good things which the Lord your God promised concerning you have been fulfilled for you, so the Lord will bring upon you all the evil things, until he have destroyed you from off this good land which the Lord your God has given you' (Jos 23.15).

Plate 86. Fully 40 metres (130 ft) above the *Wâdi Waqqâs* in the foreground rises the tell of the same name. It is longitudinal in shape, about 600 metres (1,970 ft) long, averages 200 metres (650 ft) across, and is thus larger than that of Megiddo. Behind it, to the north, can be seen a plateau of roughly 1,000 metres by 700 metres (3,280 by 2,300 ft), with steep valleys behind and to the right. It is protected to the left by an artificial canal and an enormous earth wall, the base of which is 100 metres (330 ft) thick in places. The English head of the Department of Antiquities, founded in 1920, identified this place with the ancient Hazor, made some investigations in 1928, and announced the plateau to be a fortified camp of the kind also found at Qatna and Carchemish. Since 1955 annual excavations have been made here under the leadership of Yigael Yadin, at both ends of the tell itself and at various places in the so-called camp. This proved indeed to be an extensive city destroyed shortly before 1200 B.C. Hazor is the only Palestinian city occurring in the archives of Mari (*c.* 1700 B.C.). It is found on the lists of the Pharaohs from Thothmes III onwards and is mentioned as a fortified city in the Amarna archives. Thanks in part to its excellent position on the great highway from Damascus and Mesopotamia to Egypt it was, as Joshua says (11.10), the principal royal city of the region.

Plate 87. The excavation of the eastern part of the tell in 1957; the building with the two-metres-high (6½-ft) pillars dates from the time of Ahab. Below, left, are the foundations of the gate building dating from the time of Solomon, exactly resembling that of Megiddo (cf. 1 K 9.15).

Within this impressive framework the composers of the epic brought together all kinds of traditional material of ancient and more recent date, giving little thought to the question of whether or not it all fitted in with the historical background. It is, for example, now almost certain that a number of the cities allotted to Judah in Joshua 15 did not yet exist in Joshua's day: in order to fill out the bare statement 'Judah obtained this particular region' the compilers used an administrative list dating from the time of Judah's kings. They also used older sources from which it appears that some tribes had great difficulty in taking possession of Canaanite cities (see Jos 17.11–13; cf. Jg 1.27–35). It apparently did not worry them that these details were in direct contradiction to their idea that Joshua personally conquered all the cities. We can see that the Bible text itself brings up the question of how exactly the settlement in Canaan took place. The theories proposed by scholars are still widely divergent. From the fact that no mention is made of a campaign in central Palestine and from the certainly ancient fact of the renewal of the tribal alliance at Shechem, the heart of this region (Jos 24), they conclude that the newcomers found related tribes there. Had these arrived from Egypt before them or had they never been there at all? In both cases then the idea of the twelve tribes entering together through the Jordan near Jericho must be the result of simplification. The same is true of many chapters in the Pentateuch dealing with the journey through the desert. Moreover, there are indications that the tribe of Judah contained groups which had penetrated into Canaan from the south. This confirms the impression that the entry of the tribes was in reality a very complex event. In the following chapter we shall see that archaeology has made the problem more complicated rather than solved it, which warns us to be cautious about putting too much faith in the theory that the excavations bear out the facts of the Bible.

From Joshua to Saul

According to some archaeologists, the Biblical account of a wholesale destructive invasion of the Israelites in Canaan is confirmed by traces of the simultaneous destruction of Bethel, Lachish, and *Tell Beit Mirsim* (probably Debir), occurring some time before 1200 B.C. This conviction is in some measure supported by the testimony of the Israelite archaeologists who have been working on a large scale and very ably since 1955 at Hazor in the north (Plates 86–7). On the other side of the scale, however, must be accounted the negative results obtained in Jericho and Ai. The lower layers of Jericho, which have been investigated

Plate 88. View from the overgrown ruins of Megiddo looking NE. Across the plain of Jezreel can be seen Mount Tabor to the right and to the left of it the hills of Lower Galilee.

Plate 89. The top of Mount Tabor from an aeroplane (see Plate 19 for a view from the tower of the Latin basilica on the summit right across the Greek monastery). Below the two buildings are the ruins of earlier churches and houses.

in annual campaigns since 1952 by Miss Kenyon, appear to contain settlements from the eighth millennium B.C., which means that Jericho is the oldest known city in the world. No certain trace, however, has yet been found of a Jericho dating from the thirteenth century B.C. or thereabouts. The town of Ai, whose conquest is described in Joshua 8, has long been localized in the immense ruin hill a mile and a half south-east of Bethel. It is known to the inhabitants as *et-Tell*, 'the tell', which agrees with the Hebrew name meaning 'heap of rubble'. This tell was excavated in the years 1933–4 and it was found that the site was already inhabited *c.* 3300 B.C., was completely destroyed *c.* 2400 B.C. and remained a heap of ruins until *c.* 1000 B.C., when the Israelites settled there. In Joshua's time Ai was thus what its name implies, a heap of ruins. How is this to be reconciled with the Bible? We give here four solutions proposed: (*a*) the story in Joshua 8 originated much later in order to explain the presence of the immense heap of rubble; (*b*) it possesses a core of historical truth, for the inhabitants of nearby Bethel had entrenched themselves in Ai against the invading Israelites; (*c*) the story originally concerned the conquest of Bethel, but when this town later became a flourishing Israelite city, Ai was made the subject of the narrative; and finally (*d*) Ai must be localized, not in *et-Tell*, but elsewhere. It is in any case clear that for the precise circumstances of Israel's settlement in Canaan one must fall back on conjecture. It is perhaps best to hold a middle view between a 'blitzkrieg' under Joshua, followed by total occupation, and a lengthy peaceful penetration.

Certainly the next two centuries lived on in the memory of Israel as the heroic period. The hero Joshua, whose original name, Hoshea, according to Numbers 13.16, was changed by Moses to an explicitly 'Yahwistic' form, 'Yahweh is salvation', or 'grant salvation' (pronounced 'Jesus' by the Alexandrian Jews), was followed by a number of heroic popular leaders who indeed brought 'salvation', that is victory over the enemy, release from

Plate 90. A Philistine and a Semite, detail from a relief which shows bound prisoners being brought before Rameses III. From his temple at Thebes.

Plate 91. Bronze idols from Canaan; these idols often still bear traces of gold leaf.

oppression, peace, and prosperity. The compilers of the national epic under King Josiah (see p. 114) gathered together a number of traditions concerning these figures in the present book of Judges. They thought best to serve their contemporaries, who had suffered the oppression of the Assyrians, by constantly emphasizing in this narrative series the underlying causes: it was Yahweh, their God, who, on account of the defection of the Israelites, was compelled to deliver them up to the oppressor. When in their

Plate 92. The village of *Jeba'*, the Biblical Geba, 9 km (6 miles) NNW of old Jerusalem. The shadow to the upper right is that of the deep pass on the other side of which lies the village of *Mukhmâs*, the Biblical Michmash.

Plate 93. Entrance to the pass between Geba and Michmash, the scene of Jonathan's heroic deed (see 1 S 14.4–5).

Plate 94. The plain of Jezreel. Left, the *Jebel Dahi*, probably identical with the hill of Moreh of Jg 7.1; right, the mountain range of Gilboa; between the two the plain slopes down to the Jordan. There lies Beth-shan. The Transjordan highland can just be seen in the distance. The numbers indicate the following Biblical places: 1 = En-dor; 2 = Nain; 3 = Shunem; 4 = Jezreel.

need they turned to Him again, He sent them a bringer of salvation, a 'redeemer', in the person of a judge. Notwithstanding their desire to transmit the lessons of history (cf. the prologue, Jg 2.6–3.4 and for example 10.6–16) the compilers respected the original material. Thus the modern historian can find in their works reliable information concerning the life of the tribes during these centuries. They formed a sort of sacral confederation, probably of the type also found in Greece: living about a sanctuary recognized by all, each tribe had in turn to attend to the sacrificial cult for a month. This seems to be the origin of the division into twelve tribes, in Israel and also among some neighbouring peoples (cf. the twelve 'sons' of Nahor and of Ishmael, Gn 22.20–24 and 25.13–16). After Gilgal, Shiloh, where the Ark of the Covenant was kept, functioned as the central sanctuary and also as a place of pilgrimage.

The principal campaigns of the Judges against foreign oppressors are broadly indicated on Map 4. In the north we find that of Deborah and Barak against Canaanite city rulers, where the mighty Mount Tabor (Plates 88–9) served as a rallying point. The poetical account of this struggle (Jg 5), probably composed while the events were fresh in the memory (*c.* 1125 B.C.) and transmitted almost unchanged, tells us a great deal about the common faith and inter-tribal relations. Also indicated are Gideon's action against camel-riding nomads from the east who made destructive raids into Israelite territory, Jephthah's action against the Ammonites, and Ehud's struggle against Moabite oppressors.

The greatest obstacle to the further development of the tribes of Israel was the Philistines. This people, who had taken part in the great migration which around 1200 B.C. had caused a great upheaval in all the eastern parts of the Mediterranean, and whom Rameses III (1197–1165) had with difficulty prevented from entering Egypt, had settled on the southern coastal plain. After a few decades of continual skirmishing with the nearest Israelites (this was the background which gave rise to popular tales like those concerning Samson and his famous exploits) these uncircumcised non-Semites began to penetrate farther into the central mountainous country. Superior in their knowledge of the use of iron, which they had brought with them from their land of origin (Kaftor, said the Israelites, i.e. perhaps the cultural centre, Crete), they truly terrorized the Israelites. The gripping narrative series which the compilers of the great chronicle (see p. 114) assembled in the first book of Samuel clearly shows how critical the situation was when the Ark of the Covenant, symbol of the unity of the tribes, was captured by the Philistines and when the latter occupied a large area of Israelite territory. Even the common pilgrimage centre of Shiloh was then destroyed. In reading the first book of Samuel the imagination may be supplemented by the certainly accurate portrait of a Philistine and a Semitic inhabitant of Canaan (Plate 90) and also by a photograph of the pass between Michmash and Geba, the scene of Jonathan's heroic deed (Plates 92–3). Finally, to illustrate the last chapter of 1 Samuel, there is the view of the mountains of Gilboa (Plate 94). Here Israel was crushingly defeated and Saul, her first king, slain.

The Maps

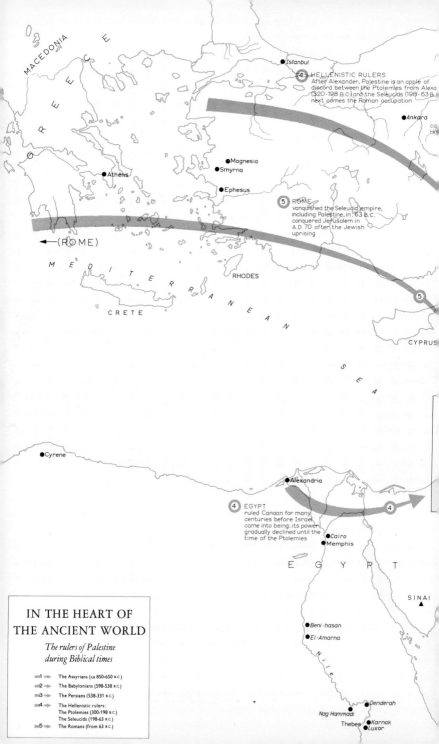

MACEDONIA

G R E E C E

● Istanbul

▣ 4 ► HELLENISTIC RULERS
After Alexander, Palestine is an apple of
discord between the Ptolemies from Alexa
(320-198 B.C.) and the Seleucids (198-63 B.
next comes the Roman occupation

● Ankara   ca
                           H(

● Magnesia
● Smyrna

● Athens

● Ephesus

⑤ ROME
vanquished the Seleucid empire,
including Palestine, in 63 B.C.,
conquered Jerusalem in
A.D. 70 after the Jewish
uprising

←— (ROME)

M E D I T E R R A N E A N

S E A

⑤

RHODES

C R E T E

CYPRUS

● Cyrene

● Alexandria

④ EGYPT
ruled Canaan for many
centuries before Israel
came into being; its power
gradually declined until the
time of the Ptolemies

④

● Cairo
● Memphis

E G Y P T

SINAI ▲

N i l e

● Beni-hasan

● El-Amarna

IN THE HEART OF
THE ANCIENT WORLD

*The rulers of Palestine
during Biblical times*

▬1 ► The Assyrians (ca 850-650 B.C.)
▬2 ► The Babylonians (598-538 B.C.)
▬3 ► The Persians (538-331 B.C.)
▬4 ► The Hellenistic rulers:
         The Ptolemies (300-198 B.C.)
         The Seleucids (198-63 B.C.)
▬5 ► The Romans (from 63 B.C.)

● Denderah

Nag Hammadi

Thebes ● Karnak
       ● Luxor

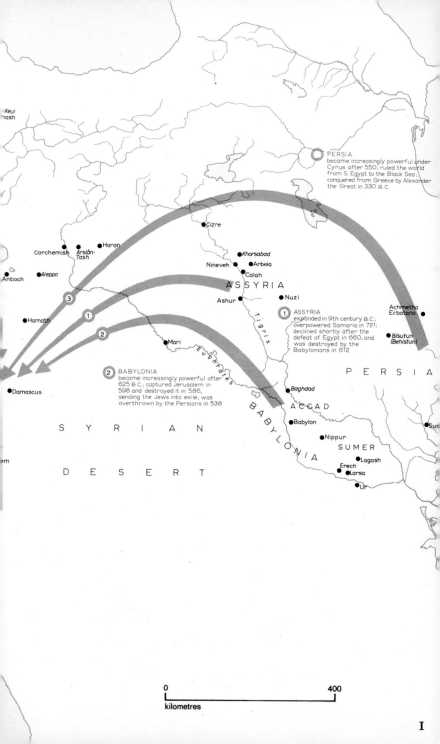

PERSIA
became increasingly powerful under Cyrus after 550; ruled the world from S. Egypt to the Black Sea, conquered from Greece by Alexander the Great in 330 B.C.

① ASSYRIA
expanded in 9th century B.C.; overpowered Samaria in 721; declined shortly after the defeat of Egypt in 660, and was destroyed by the Babylonians in 612

② BABYLONIA
became increasingly powerful after 625 B.C.; captured Jerusalem in 598 and destroyed it in 586, sending the Jews into exile; was overthrown by the Persians in 538

ASSYRIA

PERSIA

ACCAD

BABYLONIA

SUMER

S Y R I A N

D E S E R T

•Keui hash

Carchemish •Arslân-Tash •Haran

Antioch

•Aleppo

③

①

•Hamath

②

•Damascus

em

•Cizre

•Khorsabad
Nineveh• •Arbela
         •Calah
•Ashur   •Nuzi

Mari•

Tigris

Euphrates

Baghdad

•Babylon

•Nippur

Erech• •Lagash
  •Larsa
    •Ur

Achmetha
Ecbatana•

•Bisutun
(Behistun)

•Su

0   400
kilometres

I

PALESTINE

Geographical survey showing the most important excavations

- - - - - - Courses of principal highways (generalised)

Dan

UPPER GALILEE

Lake Huleh · 6 ft.

Hazor III

Acco

(HAIFA)
T. Abu Hawâm II

CARMEL

LOWER GALILEE

Capernaum

SEA OF GALILEE
- 700 ft

BASHAN

Nazareth

TABOR

Yarmuk

Caesarea III

PLAIN OF JEZREEL

Megiddo I, II

Taanach I

GILBOA

Beth-shan II

Dothan III

G R E A T

S E A

PLAIN OF SHARON

Samaria I, II

Tirzah III

Shechem II, III

Gerc

Jal
Penuel

T. el-Qasileh III

EPHRAIM

Jaffa

Shiloh II

Baal-hazor

Jordan

Gezer I, II

Mizpah II
Geba

Jericho I, II, III

Ekron

Gibeon III

Ami

Ashdod

Jerusalem

Teleilât el-Ghassûl II

Bethlehem

Kh. Qumrân III

Ashkelon

J U D A H

HILL COUNTRY

WILDERNESS

DEAD

Gaza
Tel-'Ajjûl II

P H I L I S T I A

T. el-Hesy I

Lachish II

LOWLAND

Hebron

SEA
- 1290 ft

Dibon

T. Jemmeh II

T. Beit Mirsim II

Arnon

Tel-Fâr'ah II

Beer-sheba III

M O A B

0 ——————————— 32

kilometres

2

Sultantepe

Tarsus

Haran

Carchemish

ARAM-NAHARAIM
'Aram of the two rivers'

Pethor
home of Baalam

Home of Abraham's family.
Rebekah came from here. Jacob
stayed here for a long time with
Laban

Balih

Alalakh

Aleppo

Euphrates

Qarqar

Rås Shamra
Ugarit

Orontes

Hamath

Arvad

Qatna

Zemar

Kadesh

Arqa Sin

MEDITERRANEAN

SEA

Gebal
Byblos

LEBANON

Lebo-hamath

Ba'albek

ANTI-LEBANON

SYRO-

ARABIAN

DESERT

Sidon

HERMON

Zarephath

Tyre

Damascus

Dan

Acco

Hazor

Ashtaroth

Dor Megiddo

Edrei

Taanach

Beth-shan Ham

Dothan Pella

Busra

Salecah

Tirzah

Succoth Jabbok

Shechem

Peniel
Mahanaim
Mizpah

Joppa

CANAAN

0   80

kilometres

Gezer Jericho

Jerusalem

Bethlehem

SALT SEA

Region of the Jordan

THE WANDERINGS

OF THE

PATRIARCHS

Gaza

Gerar

Hebron

On the map are indicated:

Sharuhen

Plain of
Kiriathaim

1. The places named in the stories of Genesis 12–50

Beer-sheba

Zoar

2. A few Biblical localities lying
outside Palestine proper

NEGEB

3. Only a few of the many cities
which flourished here during the
second millennium a.c.

Rehoboth

Hazazon-tamar

In the shallowest part of the
Dead Sea are usually
located Valley of Siddim,
Sodom, Gomorrah, Admah,
Zeboim

Bozrah

East of this line the average
annual rainfall is less than 4 inches

mes of drought and
the nomads
rneyed to the fertile
Delta

Punon

CAMPAIGNS OF
JOSHUA AND
THE JUDGES

Conquest of Joshua (Jos 1-12)

Expulsion of invaders by the Judges (Jg 3-16)

Misrephoth-maim
Kedesh
Meroz
Achshaph
Hazor
Meron
Beth-anath
Acco
Chinnereth
Rehob
Aphek
Madon
JOS 11
ZEBULUN
Bethlehem
TABOR
Shimron
Harosheth-ha-golim
Jokneam
Hill of Moreh
DEBORAH BARAK
Dor
Kamon
Megiddo
ISSACHAR
Jephthah summoned from Tob
GIDEON
Abel-meholah
Jabesh-gilead
Thebez
Beth-shittah
Hepher
Tirzah
EBAL
Shechem
Gathering of the tribes (Jos 24)
Succoth
Penuel
GERIZIM
Pirathon Abdon
Judges here
Arumah
Mizpah of Gilead
Aphek
EPHRAIM
Tappuah
Adam
JEPHTHAH
Lebonah
Shiloh Central sanctuary
Timnath-serah
Bethel Ai Rimmon
Beth-horon Beeroth
JOS 8
Mizpah
JOS 1-6
Gezer
JOS 9
Aijalon Chephirah Gibeon
Jericho
Abel-shittim
SAMSON
Eshtaol Kiriath-jearim
BENJAMIN
Gilgal
Ashdod
Timnah Zorah
Gibeah
Beth-jeshimoth
Hesh
Libnah
Jerusalem
JOS 10
EHUD
Makkedah
NEBO
Ashkelon
Azekah Jarmuth
Bethlehem
Gath
Adullam
HILL COUNTRY
Lachish
Gaza
Hebron
J U D A H
Jahaz
Debir
An
Anab
M O A B
Arad
Beer-sheba

0   32
kilometres

4

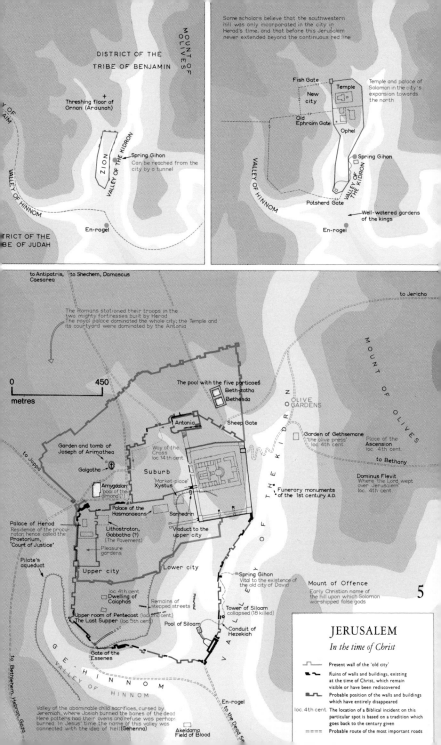

DISTRICT OF THE
TRIBE OF BENJAMIN

MOUNT OF OLIVES

✝ Threshing floor of
Ornan (Araunah)

ZION

VALLEY OF THE KIDRON

Spring Gihon
Can be reached from the
city by a tunnel

VALLEY OF HINNOM

En-rogel

DISTRICT OF THE
TRIBE OF JUDAH

Some scholars believe that the southwestern
hill was only incorporated in the city in
Herod's time, and that before this Jerusalem
never extended beyond the continuous red line

Fish Gate
Temple

New
city

Temple and palace of
Solomon in the city's
expansion towards
the north

Old
Ephraim Gate
Ophel

VALLEY OF HINNOM

VALLEY OF THE KIDRON

Spring Gihon

Potsherd Gate

Well-watered gardens
of the kings

En-rogel

to Antipatris, to Shechem, Damascus
Caesarea

to Jericho

The Romans stationed their troops in the
two mighty fortresses built by Herod.
The royal palace dominated the whole city; the Temple and
its courtyard were dominated by the Antonia

MOUNT OF OLIVES

0   450
metres

The pool with the five porticoes
Beth-zatha
Bethesda

OLIVE GARDENS

Antonia
Sheep Gate

Garden and tomb of
Joseph of Arimathea

Golgotha

Way of the
Cross
loc 14th cent

Suburb

Garden of Gethsemane
'the olive press'
loc. 4th cent.

Place of the
Ascension
loc. 4th cent.

to Bethany

Amygdalon
pool of the almond

'Market-place'
Xystus

Palace of the
Hasmonaeans

Sanhedrin

Dominus Flevit
Where 'the Lord, wept
over Jerusalem'
loc. 4th cent.

Funerary monuments
of the 1st century A.D.

Palace of Herod
Residence of the procu-
rator, hence called the
Praetorium,
'Court of Justice'

Lithostroton,
Gabbatha (?)
(The Pavement)

Viaduct to the
upper city

Pleasure
gardens

Pilate's
aqueduct

Upper city

Lower city

Spring Gihon
Vital to the existence of
the old city of David

Mount of Offence
Early Christian name of
the hill upon which Solomon
worshipped false gods

5

loc. 4th cent.
Dwelling of
Caiaphas

Remains of
stepped streets

Tower of Siloam
collapsed (18 killed)

Upper room of Pentecost (loc 2nd cent)
The Last Supper (loc 5th cent)

Pool of Siloam

Conduit of
Hezekiah

Gate of the
Essenes

GEHINNOM

VALLEY OF HINNOM

En-rogel

to Bethlehem, Hebron, Gaza

Valley of the abominable child sacrifices, cursed by
Jeremiah, where Josiah burned the bones of the dead.
Here potters had their ovens and refuse was perhaps
burned. In Jesus' time the name of this valley was
connected with the idea of hell. (Gehenna)

Akeldama
Field of Blood

to the Dead Sea

JERUSALEM

In the time of Christ

Present wall of the 'old city'

Ruins of walls and buildings, existing
at the time of Christ, which remain
visible or have been rediscovered

Probable position of the walls and buildings
which have entirely disappeared

loc. 4th cent. The location of a Biblical incident on this
particular spot is based on a tradition which
goes back to the century given

Probable route of the most important roads

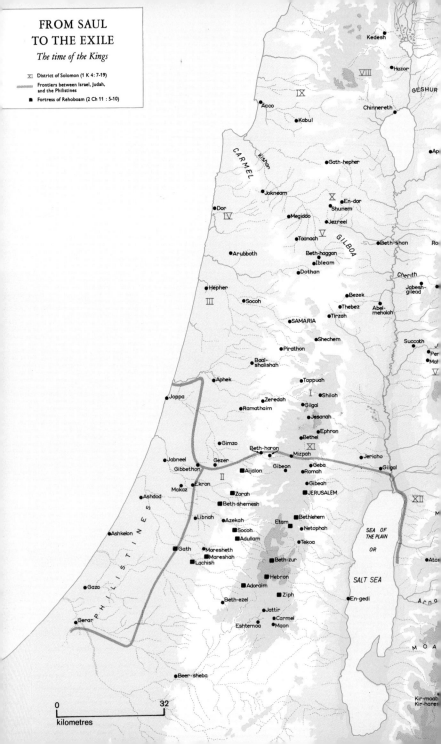

FROM SAUL
TO THE EXILE
The time of the Kings

XI   District of Solomon (1 K 4: 7-19)

━━━   Frontiers between Israel, Judah, and the Philistines

■   Fortress of Rehoboam (2 Ch 11 : 5-10)

Kedesh

Hazor

VIII

GESHUR

IX

Acco

Chinnereth

Kabul

CARMEL

Kishon

Gath-hepher

Joknearm

X

En-dor

Shunem

Dor

IV

Megiddo

Jezreel

Ap

Taanach

GILBOA

Beth-shan

Ro

Arubboth

Beth-haggan

Ibleam

Cherith

Dothan

Jabesh-gilead

Hepher

III

Bezek

Socoh

Thebez

Abel-meholah

SAMARIA

Tirzah

Succoth

J

Shechem

Per

Mah

Pirathon

V

Baal-shalishah

Tappuah

Aphek

I

Shiloh

Joppa

Zeredah

Gilgal

Ramathaim

Jesanah

Ephron

Bethel

Gimzo

Mizpah

XI

Jericho

Beth-horon

Geba

Jabneel

Gezer

Gibeon

Ramah

Gilgal

Gibbethon

II

Aijalon

Ekron

Gibeah

Makaz

Zorah

JERUSALEM

Ashdod

Beth-shemesh

PHILISTINES

Libnah

Azekah

Bethlehem

Etam

Netophah

Socoh

Adullam

SEA
OF
THE PLAIN
OR

Gath

Moresheth

Tekoa

Mareshah

Lachish

Beth-zur

Gaza

Adoraim

Hebron

SALT SEA

Ata

Beth-ezel

Ziph

En-gedi

Jattir

Arno

Carmel

Eshtemoa

Maon

MO A

Beer-sheba

Kir-moab
Kir-hares

Gerar

0   32

kilometres

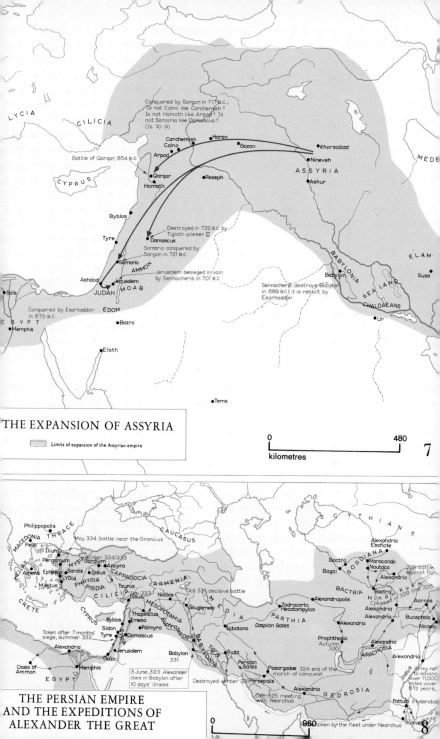

LYCIA

CILICIA

Battle of Qarqar, 854 B.C.

CYPRUS

Conquered by Sargon in 717 B.C.:
'Is not Calno like Carchemish?
Is not Hamath like Arpad? Is
not Samaria like Damascus?'
(Is 10:9)

Carchemish
Calno
Arpad
Haran
Gozan
• Khorsabad
• Nineveh
ASSYRIA
Qarqar
• Rezeph
Hamath
• Ashur

MEDE

Byblos

Tyre

Destroyed in 732 B.C. by
Tiglath-pileser III
Damascus
Samaria conquered by
Sargon in 721 B.C.
Samaria
Jerusalem besieged in vain
by Sennacherib in 701 B.C.

AMMON
Ashdod
Jerusalem
JUDAH
MOAB

ELAM

BABYLONIA
Babylon
• Susa

Sennacherib destroys Babylon
in 689 B.C. it is rebuilt by
Esarhaddon

SEA LAND
CHALDAEANS

• Ur

• Sais

Conquered by Esarhaddon
in 670 B.C.
EDOM

E G Y P T
• Memphis
• Bozra

• Elath

• Tema

THE EXPANSION OF ASSYRIA

Limits of expansion of the Assyrian empire

0   480

kilometres

7

SCYTHIANS

Philippopolis
MACEDONIA
Pella
THRACE
CAUCASUS
May 334: battle near the Granicus

Ilium
Pergamum
Gordium
HELLAS
Athens
Ephesus
Sardis
Ipsus
Ancyra
CAPPADOCIA
ARMENIA
Miletus
LYDIA
PHRYGIA
PISIDIA
Taurus
CILICIA
Issus
Nisibis
Oct 331 decisive battle
MEDIA
Gaugamela

CRETE
CYPRUS
Byblos
Sidon
Thapsacus
Emesa
Palmyra
MESOPOTAMIA
Nov 333
Damascus
Ecbatana
Caspian Gates

Alexandria Eschate
SOGDIANA
Bactra
Bagai
Maracanda
Nautaca
Alexandria
326 battle
against Porus
BACTRIA
Alexandropolis
Aornos
Hindu Kush
Alexandria
Alexandria
Bucephala
Nicaea

Taken after 7 months'
siege, summer 332
Alexandria
Tyre
Jerusalem
Gaza
Oasis of
Ammon
Memphis
E G Y P T

Babylon
331
3 June, 323: Alexander
dies in Babylon after
10 days' illness
Destroyed winter 331
Susa
Persian
Gates
Persepolis
Dec 325 meeting
with Nearchus
Pasargadae 324: end of the
march of conquest

Zadracarta
Hecatompylos
PARTHIA
Prophthasia
Autumn
330
ARACHOSIA
Alexandria

Indus
Army ref
to advance
over 11,000
miles cover
8½ years
Pattala (Hyderabad)
GEDROSIA
Alexandria

Taken by the fleet under Nearchus

THE PERSIAN EMPIRE
AND THE EXPEDITIONS OF
ALEXANDER THE GREAT

0   960

8

PALESTINE
IN THE GOSPELS
AND ACTS

Provincial boundary (approximate)

Mar Saba Modern Arabic name

PHOENICIA

GAULA

Ptolemais Ac 21:7

GALILEE

Main centre of the
preaching of Jesus

Chorazin

Beth-saida
(Julias)

Capernaum
Mt 4:13

Cana
Jn 2:1

Magdala

Lake
of
Gennesaret

Tiberias

Hippos

Kafr Kenna

SYRO

Nazareth Mt 2:23

TABOR

Gadara

Nain Lk 7:11

DECAPO

Federation of ten
Hellenistic cities

Caesarea

Residence of the
Roman procurators
Ac 10

Scythopolis

Pella

Salim(?) Jn 3:23

PLAIN OF SHARON

SAMARIA

Sebaste
the former Samaria

Sychar
Jacob's Well
Jn 4

Ac 9:35

GERIZIM

Antipatris Ac 23:31

Alexandrium

Joppa Ac 9:11

Arimathea
home of Joseph, a member
of the council
Mt 27:57

PERAE
'beyond the Jordan'

Lydda Ac 9:32

Ephraim Jn 11:54

Jericho

Jamnia

Emmaus(?) Lk 24:13

Ashdod Ac 8:40
(Azotus)

JERUSALEM
Bethany

Kh Qumrân

Ashkelon

Bethlehem

Mar Saba

J U D A E A

Herodium

DEAD

Gaza Ac 8:26

Hebron

SEA

Machaerus
Mk 6:14-26

also called
the
Asphalt Lake

Masada

0   32

kilometres

Beer-sheba

I D U M A E A

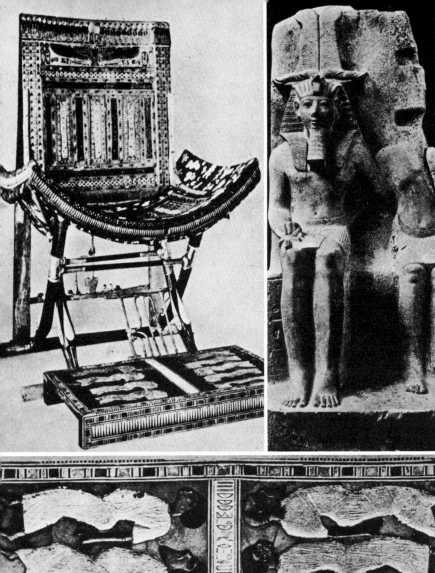

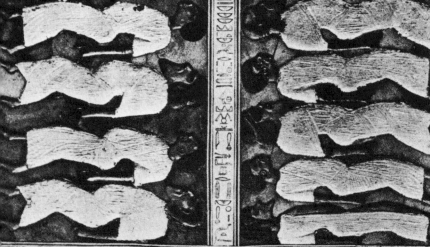

Jerusalem – City of David and of God

After the tragic death of King Saul upon the mountains of Gilboa David, until that time a vassal of the Philistines at Ziklag and at the same time the firm defender of the Judaean farmers in the frontier regions, was in Hebron proclaimed king of the tribe of Judah and anointed. He thereby reaped the reward of a shrewd and patient policy which he continued to pursue throughout the coming years in his dealings with the rest of Saul's kingdom. Finally, envoys from the northern tribes came to Hebron to ask if he would be their king. When David consented and was anointed king of all Israel *c*. 1000 B.C. he inaugurated a new era in the history of Yahweh's people.

Plate 95. A throne from the tomb of Tutankhamon. This Pharaoh, who abandoned the 'heresy' of his predecessor and father-in-law Akhenaton and returned to Thebes, was buried after his short reign (1358–1349 B.C) with magnificent treasures by the grateful priests in the Valley of the Kings. The throne, made of precious woods and inset with ivory and gold, has a footstool on which the nine traditional enemies of Egypt are depicted – in this connection we must remember that to the Egyptians anything depicted was considered in a certain sense to be really present.

Plate 96. Thothmes III sitting at the right hand of the supreme god of Thebes, Amon, whose statue was originally larger than that of the Pharaoh. It fell victim, however, to Akhenaton's religious fervour and was so badly damaged that the later restoration, in which the god was made smaller, could not stand the test of time.

Plate 97. The footstool shown in Plate 95; the text in the middle begins at the top and reads: 'All lands, every foreign land, the chiefs of the whole of Retenu as one under our two sandals equal [under] Re for ever'. Retenu is an Egyptian name for the coastal region of Syria and Palestine; Re is the sun god.

It was David who transformed the sacral tribal alliance into an important kingdom, thereby enriching Israel's religious life with new perspectives and new forms of expression. For at that time a nation's king was considered a sacral figure, a representative on earth of the national god, very closely linked with him and often even called a 'son' of the god. This conception was strong in Egypt, and David's kingship appears to have been especially influenced from this direction. According to an old tradition which is again finding credence among an increasing number of modern scholars, it was David himself to whom one of the court poets addressed the words of Psalm 110: 'The Lord says to my lord: "Sit at my right hand till I make your enemies your footstool." ' In another text the king himself says that Yahweh spoke to him: 'You are my son, today I have begotten you' (Ps 2.7). To address such words to a man, a farmer's son from Bethlehem, was unheard of in Israel, but in Egypt it was customary. For an illustration of the second text compare the obelisk of Hatshepsut (see p. 62). Both sections of the verse taken from Psalm 110 are illustrated by a picture of Thothmes III seated at the right hand of the god Amon (Plate 96), and a throne of Tutankhamon of which the footstool shows the nine traditional enemies of Egypt (Plates 95 and 97).

These few examples taken from the abundant material raise the question of how such Egyptian influences penetrated the office and undoubtedly also the ceremonial of the young royal court. The historical information which the Bible has preserved concerning David and his work is plentiful and valuable but yet not sufficient to provide a definite answer to a modern historical query. The wealth of information must be attributed to the fact that David himself was an extraordinarily fascinating person.

Plate 98. Entrance to the water tunnel of Gibeon directly behind the city wall, whose foundations can be seen.

Plates 99–100. Two water tunnels. 99: that of Gibeon. 100: that of Jerusalem, built under King Hezekiah (2 K 20.20). Its course – 510 metres (560 yds) – is given on Map 5. It carried the water from the Spring Gihon to a pool in a later part of the city which lay well within the walls.

Even during his lifetime stories grew up around him, mostly about his youth and his activities under Saul. A number of these stories are incorporated in the books of Samuel although the compiler did not trouble overmuch about the logical connection of the recorded events.

In his later years too the figure of David remained so enthralling that a learned and wise man from his entourage was inspired to write a sort of biography. The strong and sober style of this genuine masterpiece and above all the feeling for the human element, incorporated almost unchanged in the national chronicle (2 S 9–20 and 1 K 1, 2), render it far superior to any other biographical work of that period or of long afterwards. The author wrote this work during Solomon's reign. His main theme was obviously the establishment of David's dynasty; how, after many complications and setbacks, the great ruler finally obtained his successor in Solomon. That this question was of immense national and thus religious importance is obvious to anyone who carefully studies the promises made by the God of Israel to David and his house, transmitted to him by the prophet Nathan and, judging from various psalms, regularly commemorated in the religious ceremonial (2 S 7; cf. Ps 89, 132, etc.). One result of this limited aim is that this magnificent story tells us as little as the more popular traditions about what we should really like to know: how David extended and consolidated his power, how he administered and regulated the economy of his kingdom, what foreign influences there were at court, etc. The modern historian can only give an incomplete answer to these queries, gleaned from scattered notes (e.g. concerning David's conquests in 2 S 8) and casual remarks in the Biblical books themselves, from non-

Plate 101. The walls of the city which lay on the *Tell en-Nasbeh*, 11 km (8 miles) north of Jerusalem, after a sketch made by the excavators, who think that the important city of Mizpah may well lie here.

Plate 102. Sketch of a water tunnel: behind the city wall (here partly omitted) begins the tunnel which leads to the space in which the water bubbles up out of the ground (near 2); the low entry from outside could be closed with a stone in such a way that no enemy could force it (above 1). For the excess water a narrow exit was made elsewhere.

Biblical material (objects, pictures, and texts), and many hypotheses.

One important measure should be singled out in this short survey. When he accepted the kingship of the northern tribes, one enclave remained between their region and the land of Judah, the city of Jerusalem with its surrounding territory. The Philistines, alarmed by the sudden increase in power of their former vassal, gathered there with a great army in order to overpower him on his first journey to the north. David defeated them near Baal-perazim, slightly north-west of Jerusalem, and so decisively that they never again constituted a serious threat to Israel. Three centuries later Isaiah commemorated this victory as a mighty work of God (Is 28.21). David then abolished the enclave. The small but strong citadel of Jerusalem lay upon a mountain ridge, both sides of which were extremely steep. At the foot the spring Gihon had its source. In case of siege the inhabitants could cut off the access to this spring from the valley and reach the water from within the city by means of a tunnel hewn out of the rock (see the sketch, Plate 102), a system that was also applied in other towns of Canaan, in Megiddo, Gezer, and Gibeon (Plates 98–9), and which was later perfected in Jerusalem by King Hezekiah (Plate 100).

Thanks to a daring exploit by Joab, who, if we read the text aright, crept up through the water tunnel – in Jerusalem part of it was a vertical well! – and surprised the defenders (2 S 5.8; 1 Ch 11.6), David conquered the citadel. He at once made Jerusalem, of old also called Zion, the capital of his kingdom. Formerly a dividing wall between Judah and the other tribes, this city, captured by David himself and thus called by his name (see 2 S 12.28), was to become the central point of the new state of the twelve tribes. For this reason David quickly transferred there the

Plate 103. View northwards through the Kidron valley. Right, against the Mount of Offence, on the slope which in the time of the Kings contained many rock tombs, is the modern village of *Silwân* (the name reminds us of Siloam). In the background is the high temple terrace.

Plate 104. Photograph taken in almost the same direction but from the air.

Ark of the Covenant which throughout the preceding troubled years had remained half forgotten in Kiriath-jearim. Thus did the 'city of David' take over the role of ancient Shiloh which for fully a century and a half had been the centre of the tribal federation.

From the point of view of world history the importance of these first acts of David's reign can scarcely be over-estimated. One has only to consider the full import of the ideas which became linked for good at that moment of history: the God of Israel came to dwell in the city of 'his Anointed' as David's title was, *Messiah* in Hebrew, *Christos* in Greek. Ruling from God's capital this Christos had the task of ruling justly and, by settling all disputes, of causing righteousness to reign first in his own kingdom and then beyond. The promises transmitted by Nathan also concerned the coming rulers from the house of David and in fact contained the seeds of Israel's hope for a 'messianic' realm of peace for the whole of mankind, an expectation expressed in so many psalms and prophecies. The centre of these prophecies is always Zion, the city of David and of God.

Under the glorious reign of David's son Solomon (*c.* 970–930 B.C.) Jerusalem was magnificently expanded to the north. There, higher than the city itself and more exposed to the wind, to make the winnowing easier (Plate 132), lay the threshing floor of Araunah (Ornan) which David had bought from this Jebusite in order to erect an altar there and to offer sacrifice. Upon this spot, with the help of architects, artists, and material from Phoenicia (including cedars from Lebanon), Solomon built a temple for

Plate 105. Aerial photograph of Jerusalem. The numbers (those in *italic* type also occur on Plate 106) are: *1* = Kidron valley; *2* = Tyropoeon valley; *3* = Spring Gihon; *4* = the Garden of Gethsemane; *5*: see description of Plate 106; *6* = the ancient road to Jericho across the slopes of the Mount of Olives; *7* = Dominus Flevit; 13 = the church above Calvary and the Holy Sepulchre; 14 = the three towers of Herod's palace; 15 = Church of the Cenacle (traditional site of the Last Supper and the miracle on Whit Sunday).

Plate 106. Aerial photograph of Jerusalem: *5* = the modern asphalt road to Jericho which runs through Bethany; *8* = the site of Bethphage; *9* = mosque on the traditional scene of the Ascension; 10 = German hospital on the site of Nob; 11 = site of the village of Bahurim (2 S 16.5); 12 = Anathoth.

Yahweh in which he placed the Ark of the Covenant. He undoubtedly enlarged the surface around the threshing floor by building an artificial terrace. We shall never know the exact dimensions of this terrace nor the exact site of the imposing palace that Solomon built between the temple and city. For Herod had the terrace enlarged into an enormous temple square. This is now the site of the Mosque of Omar, and as the deeply venerated rock is the second holy place of Islam after Mecca it has never been possible to excavate the site.

Looking northwards through the Kidron valley one can see the elevation of the terrace, the site of Solomon's palace and temple (Plate 103). It also dominates the three aerial photos of Jerusalem (Plates 104–6), which are grouped together so that, together with Map 5, they may offer a good general view of the ground relief, the historical development of the city, and the position of the principal holy places. Fortunately the description of Solomon's temple and its furniture (1 K 6–7), which is hard to understand, can now be illustrated by various archaeological discoveries. On the clear ground plan, to which a remarkable parallel was found at Hazor (Plate 107), fairly reliable reconstructions can be made (Plate 109), while the descriptions of objects for the religious ceremonies, e.g. laver and altar, can also be made clear with

Plate 107. Canaanite temple found in the most northern part of Hazor. Of the three rooms which correspond with the entrance hall, the main hall, and the rear hall (the Holy of Holies) of Solomon's temple, we see here the rear hall. The floor is strewn with religious objects and surrounded by a series of skilfully made long basalt tiles (a Hittite method of construction), on which wooden beams evidently lay to strengthen the brick wall above. The central and entrance halls are visible in the background. In front of the entrance were found two round basalt pillar bases. The temple, 25 metres (82 ft) long and 17 metres (56 ft) wide, and, judging from traces of fire, suddenly and completely destroyed around the year 1200 B.C., had thus two pillars before the entrance, exactly like the temple of Solomon.

Plate 108. Some objects used in the religious services. In front, an overturned incense altar of basalt, 1·4 metres (4½ ft) high and 50 cm (20 in.) broad. The star within a circle is the emblem of the Canaanite sun god. Also visible are two basalt slabs with rectangular hollows, obviously for the libations with the liquids (oil or wine) which were stored in the magnificent jars.

concrete examples (Plates 110–11). The same holds good for the ornamentations (Plate 112). Excavators have found remains of Solomon's constructions outside Jerusalem, at Megiddo among other places, where the city gate (see the reconstructed sketch, which shows the gate with its fortifications and buildings, Plate 113) has now an exact parallal at Hazor (Plate 87, left foreground).

Although he lost some of the regions conquered by his father, Solomon increased his wealth by large-scale world trade. His merchant fleet, built and manned by Phoenicians, sailed from the harbour near Ezion-geber on the Gulf of Elath and made journeys to the distant gold country of Ophir. The excavations at Ezion-geber even provided a supplement to the awe-inspired account in the Bible in which Solomon's glory already seems to have become legendary: the remains of a large metal industry were found there. Within a few decades, therefore, the farming people of Israel were called upon to assimilate a succession of innovations. Many of these were of foreign, mainly Egyptian, origin.

Jerusalem was an extremely old city, dependent for centuries upon the Pharaohs (like, for example, Beth-Shan; see Plate 50, bottom right), and possessing venerable religious traditions. The Bible itself records that of Melchizedek, king and priest of God Most High (Gn 14.18–24). We are not told that David killed the Jebusites and their king; on the contrary, his respect for the possession of Araunah is striking. It is possible that David, later considered as the great organizer of the temple service, adopted elements from these traditions, including some which concerned

Plate 109. Reconstruction sketch of the temple of Solomon from data supplied by G. Wright and W. F. Albright. The two pillars, called Joachim and Boaz (probably after the first words of their inscriptions), were made entirely of bronze and were over 10 metres (32 ft) high.

Plates 110–11. Objects used in religious ceremonies. 110: model of a laver on a stand, 39 cm ($15\frac{1}{2}$ in.) high, dating from the twelfth century B.C., found in a tomb in Cyprus. The ornamentation includes winged sphinxes and birds at the corners. 111: an altar from Megiddo, 55 cm ($21\frac{1}{2}$ in.) high, from a slightly later period; note the 'horn' at each corner.

Plate 113. Reconstruction drawing of one of the gates of Megiddo, fortified by Solomon.

Plate 112. Examples of carved ivory. This art flourished in Syria in the time of Israel's kings. To decorate wooden panels, chairs, couches, etc., all kinds of figures, inspired by motifs from Egypt, Mesopotamia, and the Greek islands, were carved from small ivory tablets. The pieces shown here come from Hazael's palace in Damascus (found, however, as war booty of the Assyrians of *Arslân-Tash*), from Megiddo, and from the palace of Ahab at Samaria (cf. for example Am 3.15, 6.4). One can imagine this kind of carving when reading descriptions of the decoration of Solomon's temple: 'carved figures of cherubim, and palm trees and open flowers' (1 K 6.29).

his own role as king of Yahweh's people. Certainly Egyptians and officials trained in Egypt assisted in the organization of the new kingdom. Solomon married a daughter of the Pharaoh. This being so it appears possible to form an idea of many of the activities of Solomon's court, music and dance for example, with the help of Egyptian reliefs (Plate 114).

All these innovations were bound to arouse fierce reactions among a people so attached to its traditions. Especially unpopular was the new administrative division of the kingdom into twelve districts, which Solomon introduced (see 1 K 4.7–20 and Map 6) and which deliberately severed the old tribal connections. On the other hand the political reorganization had its advantages.

Solomon was possessed of superhuman wisdom (1 K 4.29–34), and the legends about it were manifold. By 'wisdom' one must understand not only an encyclopedic and ordered knowledge of everything under the sun, but also the concise definition of all forms of human behaviour, in particular the art of being the perfect gentleman. This art, so indispensable for the attainment of a successful career, had been practised for centuries in Egypt.

The nucleus of the earliest collections of proverbs in the Bible (Pr 10–22 and 25–9) probably originated in the circles of the royal officials. These proverbs contain no mention of Israel, alliance,

Plate 114. Music and dance in ancient Egypt; relief from an unfinished temple of Hatshepsut at Karnak.

Plate 115. Relief from the mortuary chapel of Patenemheb (*c.* 1350 B.C.), now in Leiden; behind the priest, who is performing the funeral sacrifice (he is wearing an animal skin), sit four musicians with their instruments – a harp, a lute, and two flutes. The harpist 'far surpasses the others in beauty. What splendour upon a surface of a few square centimetres! The sunken features, the desolate pose, the dead eyes, it is the blind man as we have all seen him in daily life' (Guide to the Museum). Also well-known is the hieroglyphic text above the scene, in which the harpist sings of the transitoriness of all famous men and of their tombs and the inevitability of death: 'No one returns from thence to tell us what a man needs there and to calm our fears until we too arrive where they have gone before. Follow your desire as long as you live; lay myrrh upon your head and clothe yourself in fine linen. Increase your possessions and do not give way to dejection. Do what you will upon earth and do not torment your heart before the day of tears arrives . . .' (cf. Ecclesiastes).

election, holiness or the like, but during Solomon's reign or the following century a work was composed in which the deepest religious convictions of Israel were set down in an imposing manner. In a style which equals that of the already mentioned court chronicle of David but which is much more pronouncedly religious, an author (or a group of authors) laid the foundations of the so-called Yahwistic chronicle. In an attempt perhaps to preserve the old traditions of the disintegrating confederation, a coherent narrative was made of Israel's past, from Abraham to the death of Moses. It was preceded by a profound introduction which began with the general human aspect, the creation of *adam*, that is, of man, in paradise. The stories of the fall, the fratricide, the flood and the tower of Babel represented the rapid growth of evil with as a result the total disintegration of a humanity which Yahweh had intended to form a happy community. Against this background was projected the call of Abraham, that is, of Israel: through him Yahweh wished to make mankind one again and to heap humanity with blessings.

Plates 116–17. 116: Canaanite ruler; detail from an ivory tablet (Plate 117), 26 cm (10 in.) long, found at Megiddo. Judging from the holes (see Plate 117) it was mounted on some object (a sheath?). The King, drinking from a bowl and reaching with his other hand for a lotus flower, sits upon a throne supported by two winged animals with human heads, the cherubim, perhaps an illustration of the cherubim on which the divine ruler of Israel was invisibly enthroned in the Holy of Holies. The woman before him who is handing him the lotus appears to be offering a piece of her shawl as a napkin. On the rather indistinct Plate 117, a figure can be seen behind her playing a nine-stringed lyre (as David did before Saul); then follow naked prisoners walking bound before an officer riding in a war chariot with two horses in front of it and the winged sun floating above.

Judah and Israel

Immediately after Solomon's death, *c.* 930 B.C., the inner cleavage of the Kingdom, already obvious at times under David, and aggravated by Solomon's manner of ruling, expressed itself by a split. Then the old cry was heard again in the North: 'What portion have we in David? We have no inheritance in the son of Jesse. To your tents, O Israel!' (1 K 12.16; cf. 2 S 20.1). The rebels, assembled in the ancient meeting place of Shechem, chose as king a certain Jeroboam. A born leader, this man of the tribe of Ephraim had been appointed by Solomon as chief inspector of the forced labour carried out by 'the house of Joseph', which included not only Ephraim and Manasseh but all the northern tribes. On account of his revolutionary tendencies he had been obliged to hide in Egypt from the king's police. According to 1 Kings 11 these tendencies had been strengthened in him by Ahijah, a prophet from Shiloh, the old religious centre of the tribal alliance, also in Ephraim. Designated by a prophet and proclaimed by the people, just as Saul and David had been, Jeroboam began to rule as king in Shechem.

The Disruption was never to be healed, and from now on the northerners, with Jeroboam as their king, can be called Israel, as distinct from Judah over which Solomon's son Rehoboam ruled as king.

The political division was of course accompanied by a religious one. Jeroboam appointed two sanctuaries in his kingdom for the worship of Yahweh, one of them in the north, in Dan, the other in Bethel, 15 km (9½ miles) north of Jerusalem. Its foundation was attributed to the patriarch Jacob, also called Israel. In both

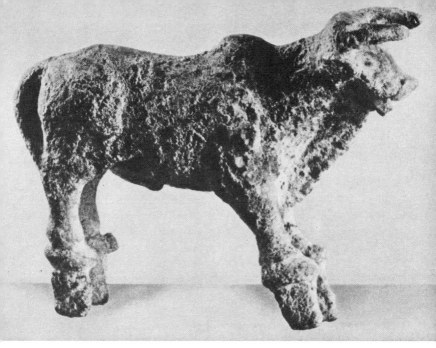

Plate 118. Small bronze statue of a bull from Hazor.

Dan and Bethel the King caused to be set up the statue of a bull-calf, covered in gold. This animal had been from ancient times a popular symbol of the divinity who grants life and fruitfulness. Recently a small statue of a bull was found in a pre-Israelite sanctuary in Hazor (Plate 118). Jeroboam sought in this way to render the worship of Yahweh more attractive. Perhaps he meant these statues to be the pedestals upon which Yahweh, the giver of all fertility, is invisibly enthroned. In the region around Canaan several pictures have been found representing a divinity standing upon the animal linked with him (see the left of Plate 50). Sometimes their likeness is replaced by a symbol, for example a heavenly body, placed above the animal. But the common people in Israel would not be able to make this distinction and would begin to worship the calf as Yahweh, just as the pagans served their Baals, with profound effect upon their life and thought.

Two centuries later Isaiah, as attached to Zion, the abode of the Holy One of Israel, as to the house of David, was to consider this Disruption whereby 'Ephraim fell away from Judah' as the greatest calamity that ever befell the people of God (Is 7.17). How Yahweh judged Jeroboam's deed appeared abundantly clear to the prophet and his disciples in 721, when Assyria wiped the entire Northern Kingdom from the map. During Sennacherib's campaign against Judah in 701, only Jerusalem was spared, by a miraculous dispensation. It thus became increasingly clear that the God of Israel wished to be worshipped only in Jerusalem, nowhere else, not even upon the ancient and venerable 'high places' or local sanctuaries in the district around the capital. Although King Hezekiah took all measures to this end it was above all Josiah who carried out the evident wish of Yahweh, unambiguously expressed in the book of Deuteronomy.

The compilers of the books of Kings (the third part of the great chronicle; see p. 85) were guided by the same conviction. They derived their basic information about the history of the two kingdoms from the official royal annals or from extracts. These gave them the dates of the outline within which they dealt with every reign: 'In the . . . th year of X, King of Judah (Israel), Y became king of Israel (Judah) and ruled for . . . years'. Then follows their judgement. All the kings of Israel were reproved because they continued in the path of Jeroboam who had led Israel into sin – in other words, because they did not put an end to the division of the kingdom. This is the reason for the lesson in narrative form – rather complicated for modern readers – in 1 Kings 13 (see also 14) and the summary of 2 Kings 17. The kings of Judah were all of David's dynasty and the house of Yahweh was the royal temple of them all. And yet only eight of them were accounted good, six with the spiteful remark that under them 'the high places were not removed'. Only Hezekiah and Josiah receive unmixed praise. The convictions of the chroniclers also influenced strongly the choice of the material with which they filled in their outline. They held as especially important for contemporaries and descendants stories which had to do with religion, i.e. in which the temple played a role or a prophet appeared. We hear about the invasion of Shishak (the first

Pharaoh the Bible mentions by name) because Rehoboam paid him a ransom with treasures from the temple. We know a little more about Ahab because he is Elijah's opponent in the fine cycle of stories about this prophet. That Ahab, with 10,000 men and 2,000 war chariots, took part in the battle of Qarqar against Shalmaneser V in 854 B.C. was apparently one of the details which the reader had to look up for himself in the official chronicles, if he was interested. The annals of Judah and Israel no longer exist, but we still have those of the Assyrians, inscribed in clay and stone. It is from this source that we know that Ahab took part in this battle.

From these and other non-Biblical texts and from archaeological data the modern historian can supplement the rather biased material of Kings (and Chronicles, even more biased but with a few valuable additions), thus forming the picture of Israel now found in reliable history books. Thus, in the six lines about Omri, we are told only that he abandoned his capital of Tirzah after six years and built a new one that he called Samaria. What he began to build in Tirzah has been excavated, just beneath the surface of the tell (Plates 32–3). His palace in Samaria has also been excavated, and the remains of ivory friezes found (Plate 112). We now understand why he changed capitals and esteem him as the greatest ruler of Israel.

In reading the books of Kings Figure 5 (pp. 164–5) may prove helpful. Map 6 indicates the possible sites of most of the places mentioned in the narratives of Samuel, Kings, and Chronicles.

In the Hands of the Assyrians

Seen from the point of view of world politics Israel and Judah during the two centuries following the division of the kingdom formed part of the group of small states between the Euphrates and the Brook of Egypt which were perpetually warring with each other. In the east lay Edom, Moab, and Ammon, all formerly part of David's kingdom and independent after the division; to the north was Damascus, also once under David's rule, and farther north was Hamath. In the west were the Philistine cities with, to the north, Tyre, which dominated the coast up to Mount Carmel, Sidon, etc. We do not possess many details concerning this perpetual bickering. The fullest accounts in the Bible concern the wars between Israel and Damascus and only in so far as they form the background to the stories of Elijah and Elisha. The former strongly opposed the paganism which had penetrated the new capital of Samaria. Tirzah, which Omri abandoned in the sixth year of his reign and where archaeologists have found imposing but unfinished foundations just below the surface of the tell (Plate 33), lay at the head of a valley which opened southeastwards and formed a good link with Transjordan (Plate 119). Under Omri, however, most of it was lost to Mesha, King of Moab, who records this on his famous stele. Anyone with a knowledge of Biblical Hebrew can read this unique remnant of

Plate 119. The city of Tirzah at the head of the valley which runs in a southeasterly direction towards the valley of the Jordan (visible on the left of Plate 3).

Plate 120. The isolated hill on which King Omri built his new capital of Samaria; it later bore Herod's splendid city, Sebaste, whose name is perpetuated in the modest village of *Sebastiyeh*.

Moabite literature (a convincing proof of the strong link between Israel and Moab, see p. 91), in which Mesha gives an account of his conquests in Israel north of the Arnon. Partly in order to present a stronger front against Damascus Omri chose his new capital so as to have good lines of communication with Tyre. His son Ahab married a princess from this city. This marriage heralded the large-scale introduction of paganism that aroused the protest of Elijah. Ahab continued the struggle against Damascus, a struggle for commercial interest and the possession of Gilead with its citadel Ramoth-gilead in northern trans-Jordan. As we know from Assyrian sources fighting ceased for a time in 853.

Israel had long known that the old spirit of conquest once again prevailed in Assyria. It had also heard of the terrible methods employed by Ashurnasirpal (883–859) in his destruction of the small Aramaean states of Mesopotamia. In the name of the god Ashur, who wished to possess the whole world, his son Shalmaneser III (858–824) had added to the regions already conquered and extremely well organized by his father. He had penetrated into Cilicia and in 854 turned his armies towards the south. Near Qarqar on the Orontes, however, he was met by twelve allied kings whose names he gives, together with the contingents they brought with them. Ahab of Israel is companionably listed next to Hadadezer of Damascus! Shortly afterwards, however, they are again fighting among themselves, especially when the Assyrian menace seems to have lessened. In 841, Jehu, of whom we know so much from the stories about Elisha, the prophet who supported him in his policy, had to pay tribute to Shalmaneser, who recorded this fact upon his black obelisk, 2 metres ($6\frac{1}{2}$ ft) high, now in the British Museum. A detail from this obelisk (Plate 121) shows Israel's king (with a pointed cap) prostrating himself before the Assyrian ruler, who is pouring a libation. His gods are represented by the symbols of Ashur and Ishtar, a

Plate 121. Detail from a four-sided commemorative stele of Shalmaneser III from his palace at Calah (*Nimrûd*), now in the British Museum. According to the text (magnificently engraved cuneiform writing), it represents the offering of 'the tribute of Jehu, son of Omri'. He was, however, not a son but a usurper of the throne of this great ruler of Israel.

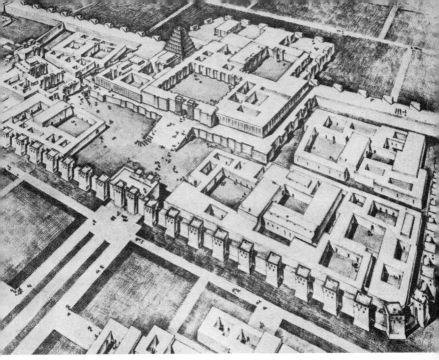

Plate 123. Reconstruction drawing by the excavators of Dur Sharrukîn, the citadel built by Sargon II and intended as the court capital. It was abandoned by his son Sennacherib in favour of Nineveh and was therefore rediscovered comparatively intact. Note the ziggurat.

winged sun and a star. On this occasion Damascus had also to pay tribute. When shortly afterwards Assyrian pressure lessened, Damascus fell upon Israel with renewed vigour. Israel's position was weakened by the fact that its relations with Tyre had been severed as a result of Elijah's protests. This struggle was brought to an end by Adad-nirari III (809–782), who dealt Damascus a crushing blow. After him, Assyria passed through a period of internal conflict. Both Israel and Judah reacted by flourishing mightily, ruled respectively by Jeroboam II (783–743) and

Plate 122. Detail of a relief, fully 90 cm (35 in.) high, from the palace of Ashurbanipal at Nineveh, now in the British Mueseum. According to the inscription at the top (not visible) the destruction of the royal city of Hamanu in Elam is depicted here.

Plate 124. King Ashurbanipal hunting wild asses; relief, 53 cm. (21 in.) high, from Nineveh, now in the British Museum.

Azariah (Uzziah) (781–740). During the latter's reign the southern kingdom grew prosperous. Lost territories were reconquered, the ring of fortresses around Jerusalem was extended and made stronger, and the army was reorganized. In addition to these military activities methods were introduced to improve farming and stock-breeding. Yet even before these kings had gone to rest with their fathers the apparently somnolent giant in the north awoke once more.

Plate 125. The storming of a city in the time of Tiglath-pileser III, now in the British Museum.

Plate 126. Deportation of the inhabitants of the city of Astartu (according to the inscription), probably the Biblical Ashtaroth, east of the Sea of Galilee. From the palace at Calah.

158

Tiglath-pileser, the greatest ruler in Assyrian history, came to the throne in 745. He inaugurated the deportation system, by which, if it had not already been exterminated, the population of a conquered city was transferred to another part of the empire and replaced by colonists from still other regions. In this way he sought to kill the nationalism of the conquered peoples and to prepare an empire in which everyone would feel at home everywhere while being everywhere subject to members of the small, proud nation of Assyria.

In 738 Tiglath-pileser began a series of campaigns against the west. In 734 he applied the deportation principle to a large section of Israel. His successor, Shalmaneser V, began a siege of Samaria. It was conquered in 721 by Sargon II and the inhabitants deported. This meant the end of the kingdom of the ten tribes. Under Sennacherib (705–681), Jerusalem barely escaped destruction. Judah might still survive, but for how long? Plate 122 is an illustration of the 'Assyrian method' found on a relief from Nineveh. While engineers tear down the outer walls of the city flames are already leaping from the citadel and the city gate. The last booty-laden soldiers have just passed through it (see p. 173), followed by a comrade driving two civilians before him. Below, a view of the army camp with soldiers and sutlers carousing. Plate 123 is a reconstruction drawing of Dur Sharrukîn, Sargon's new capital on the site of the present-day Khorsabad, and Plate 124 shows King Ashurbanipal hunting. The latter is a sample of the Assyrian mastery in the art of relief, especially in the depiction of animals. Covered battering rams on wheels (Plate 125), the precursors of our tanks, were used to storm the walls. Above, one sees inhabitants impaled upon stakes and others begging for mercy from the towers. There is also an officer (in a long skirt) drawing a bow, with a soldier next to him holding a shield taller than a man; behind them is a similar group. Plate 126 is the picture of a group of deported inhabitants with Assyrian soldiers.

Plate 127. Ashurbanipal in his state chariot; detail from a relief from Nineveh, now in the Louvre. To Isaiah the Assyrian world ruler is destructive, proud, and cruel, the opposite of the true ruler Yahweh and his Anointed.

The Prophets

Even the briefest survey of Israel's history cannot fail to mention the remarkable and, in the end, inexplicable phenomenon of Israel's prophets. Everyone remembers from the stories about Saul how, while searching for his father's asses, he meets a band of prophets in a state of exaltation and how he is carried away with them. This happens again later and afterwards Saul spends a day and a night naked upon the ground. A closer reading of these old tales reveals that this class of people, who worked themselves into a state of trance with the help of song and dance in a way that we perhaps find difficult to accept, were honoured in Israel as one of the means by which Yahweh might reveal himself. It is openly told of the great Elisha that he needed a zither player to attain the state of trance in which he transmitted the will of Yahweh. We are also told that one of Jehu's officers, speaking of a prophet of Elisha's circle, exclaimed: 'Why has this madman come to you?' King Ahab had 400 such prophets in his service and their manner of obtaining for the King a revelation in God's name concerning for example the outcome of a projected campaign will probably not have been very different from the way in which the prophets of Baal tried to extort a sign from their god upon Mount Carmel. We now know that this sort of prophecy was also known in the lands around Israel and that some kings had included prophets in their court. The remarkable thing with

Plate 128. The western spur of the Carmel range, seen from the beach of the bay of Acco. At the foot lies Haifa, founded from Tyre in the fourth century B.C. Only in recent times has it developed into one of the most important cities of Palestine.

Figure 5

THE PROPHETS 'Writing Prophets' in white on black			attacks from EGYPT	The kings of JUDAH and ISRAEL		attacks from MESOPOTAMIA
Nathan Gad				David Solomon	*italics = usurper*	
	950		Shishak (Sheshong)			
Ahijah				(Disruption 931)		
	900			Rehoboam	*Jeroboam I*	ASSYRIANS Ashurnasirpal III 883-858
Jehu				Abijam Asa	Nadab *Baasha*	
					Elah *Zimri*	
Elijah	850				*Omri*	Shalmaneser III 856-824 (battle of Qarqar 854)
				Jehoshaphat	Ahab	
Elisha				Joram Ahaziah (*Athaliah*)	Ahaziah Joram	(tribute of Jehu 841)
				Joash	*Jehu*	Shamshi-adad V 824-810
	800				Joahaz	Adad-nirari III 810-782 (tribute 805)
				Amaziah	Joash	(8 weak kings) Shalmaneser IV 781-772
Jonah				Uzziah	Jeroboam II	Ashurdan III 771-754
AMOS HOSEA	750				Zechariah	Ashur-nirari 754-746 *Tiglath-pileser III 748-727*

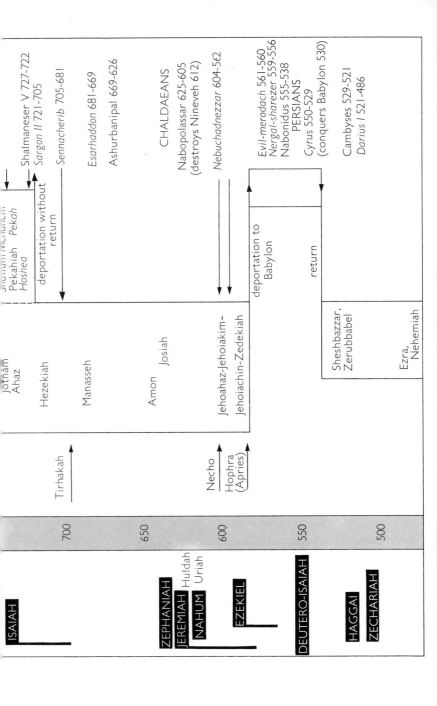

This is a historical timeline chart (rotated). Reading the content:

Rulers and events (top section):

Shalmaneser V 727-722
Sargon II 721-705
Sennacherib 705-681

Esarhaddon 681-669
Ashurbanipal 669-626

CHALDAEANS
Nabopolassar 625-605
(destroys Nineveh 612)

Nebuchadnezzar 604-562

Evil-merodach 561-560
Nergal-sharezer 559-556
Nabonidus 555-538
PERSIANS
Cyrus 550-529
(conquers Babylon 530)

Cambyses 529-521
Darius I 521-486

Israel/Judah kings (middle section):

Pekahiah   Pekah
Hoshea

deportation without return

Jotham
Ahaz
Hezekiah
Manasseh
Amon   Josiah
Jehoahaz-Jehoiakim-
Jehoiachin-Zedekiah

deportation to Babylon

return

Sheshbazzar,
Zerubbabel

Ezra,
Nehemiah

Tirhakah

Necho
*Hophra
(Apries)*

Timeline scale:

700
650
600
550
500

Prophets/books (bottom section):

ISAIAH

ZEPHANIAH   Huldah
JEREMIAH   Uriah
NAHUM

EZEKIEL

DEUTERO-ISAIAH

HAGGAI
ZECHARIAH

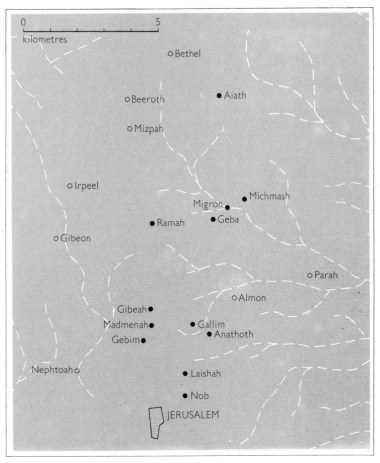

Figure 6

Israel is that time and again such groups produced men who knew, in a manner difficult to describe but with complete certainty, that the God of Israel spoke to them and appointed them to be his spokesmen. Such people are found throughout the whole period of the monarchy, from Nathan, who voiced God's displeasure over David's shameful act, to the prophet Uriah who spoke in the same spirit as Jeremiah against the 'false' prophets and paid for this outspokenness with his life. They include too

166

the 'writing prophets', so called because their words are handed down in the Biblical writings named after them. In former centuries they were involuntarily considered as theologians of a sort, gifted in addition with the ability to give particulars of the distant messianic future.

The end of the last century, however, brought a change in this manner of thinking. A careful analysis of the prophetic books showed that they had been composed long after the death of their supposed authors. They comprised fragments of their preaching, handed down orally and in writing and filled out with various texts, some of a much later date. A second reason was that modern man, with his sense of historical development and his interest in the personality of each individual, gained more understanding of the situation in which each prophet played out his role and the manner in which, in an entirely personal manner, he voiced the message of his God. It was noticed that the public activity of most of the 'writing prophets' coincided with periods of national crisis. The outline given in Figure 5 will, it is hoped, clarify this. Within the framework are the kings of Israel and Judah; to their right, the rulers of the kingdoms in Mesopotamia (the names in italics are mentioned in the Bible; the arrows indicate their principal actions). Immediately to the right of the date column are the rare actions originating from Egypt, and to the extreme left of the page the row of prophets, with the names of the writing prophets in capital letters. Towards the end of the extremely prosperous reigns of Jeroboam II and Uzziah, favoured by the weakness of Assyria, we see the first 'writing prophets' appear. Prosperity had above all profited the rich merchants and officials; they considered this as a material consequence of Israel's election, which they celebrated in the pompous religious ceremonies. They remained blind to the fact that their unjust treatment of the lower classes cried out for vengeance. In this crisis Amos, the unbending herdsman from Tekoa, proclaimed ruin and deportation in the name of Yahweh, who nowhere tolerates injustice and certainly not among the people he has chosen. 'Israel's moral decay is in reality faithlessness towards a true and honourable partner', cried Hosea shortly afterwards. This

167

prophet, abandoned by his wife yet continuing to love her, saw in the coming disasters the expression of an offended love.

In 745 Tiglath-pileser ascended the throne of Assyria and at the outset occupied himself with setting his own country in order. When, after some years, it became known in Jerusalem what this man intended to do in the name of his god Ashur, and the shrewd envisaged with dismay the possibility that Israel might soon cease to exist (and with it the dominion of Yahweh?), the well-educated and gifted Isaiah underwent in the temple of Jerusalem his well-nigh shattering experience of the most holy God of Israel, who is the unique, the only Lord, 'the' King. He dared then to announce that the world conqueror was no more than a stick caught up by the God of Israel from beyond the Euphrates to chastise His people. All the peoples of Syria and Palestine would shortly be faced with the possibility of annihilation or survival: among the people of Yahweh only those would survive who believed, that is, who trusted in him alone. The vertical stroke under Isaiah's name in our scheme indicates the length of his ministry. He lived through the destruction of Israel and Sennacherib's vain siege of Jerusalem. A century later, when the Babylonians had taken over the Assyrian empire and its deportation methods, the end dawned for Judah. Jeremiah, sensitive and lonely but in constant conversation with his God, saw the uprising under Josiah, the failure of all the latter's good measures (if Yahweh would only engrave his commandments in the heart of man!) and the end of Judah's existence as a nation. The exiles of 587 were received in Babylon by Ezekiel, the eccentric but influential saviour of the old faith in that distant land. When, around 550 B.C., the whole of Mesopotamia was in ferment over the mysterious but mighty power descending from the Persian highlands (new war, new policy, a new and universal religion!) there emerged from among the exiles the unknown poet of Isaiah 40–55, commonly called the

Plate 129. The village of '*Anâta* seen from the hill upon which lie the ruins of Jeremiah's Anathoth.

Plate 130. The spring of Parah, 5 km (3 miles) ENE of Anathoth.

second or Deutero-Isaiah, who profoundly and stirringly proclaimed the restoration of Jerusalem. Around 520 a group of returned exiles wandered disconsolately among the ruins of temple and city. Here was another crisis, and now appeared the prophets Haggai and Zechariah.

On careful study of their authentic utterances, each prophet is seen to have a distinctive, characteristic manner of speaking about God, determined as much by his education and temperament as by the circumstances in which he prophesies. Yet notwithstanding the originality of their style, strong resemblances can also be detected, not only because the later prophets build upon the preaching of their predecessors (the young Isaiah was familiar with that of Amos, Jeremiah with that of Hosea), but because they all stand upon common ground, the heritage of Moses. Half a century ago it was still customary to view the prophets as the fell opponents of all outward forms of worship and as the discoverers of the service 'in spirit and truth'. This opinion has since been rightly moderated.

Nowadays many even believe that it was precisely the religious ceremonies which, in a combination of rites, narratives, and song, had preserved the essential core of Yahwism, and which formed the starting point for the prophets of that reflection to which their inward experience impelled them.

Whoever journeys through Palestine as a pilgrim is reminded time and again of these great spokesmen of God. On his arrival in Haifa he sees in thought Elijah's servant standing upon the promontory of Carmel looking for the rain cloud (Plate 128). The visitor who has climbed the Mount of Olives near the German hospital (Plate 106, No. 10), where the small locality of Nob is sited with some degree of probability, must immediately think of the stirring poem in which Isaiah describes the Assyrian march upon Zion (Is 10.28–34, perhaps the sequel of 5.26–9). For he sees before him some of the places of which Isaiah speaks (see Figure 6; places in Isaiah 10 have black dots: some of the sites are

Plate 131. A man on a flat threshing board which is drawn by two muzzled oxen.

Plate 132. Winnowers.

uncertain). Turning, he understands how, from Nob, where he now stands, the Assyrian could shake his fist threateningly towards the hill of Zion which he sees lying below (Plate 106, No. 1). From there it is not far to the small village of 'Anâta near which lies the tell of Jeremiah's birthplace, Anathoth (Plate 129). Following a pipe-line downwards from here one comes to the brimming spring from which drinking water is pumped to Jerusalem (Plate 130). It was called Parah in Jeremiah's time and is perhaps the Perath (which usually means Euphrates) of Jeremiah 13.4–7. On the way back he may feel annoyance at a farmer who has muzzled his threshing oxen (Plate 131) contrary to the spirit of the prophets as revealed in Deuteronomy 25.4. Yet he will remember other texts upon threshing, like the moving expression used by a prophet in exile when addressing his defeated people, 'O my threshed and winnowed one' (Is 21.10). Farther on two farmers are busily tossing the threshed grain into the air: the heavy grains fall back, the chaff is scattered in the wind (Plate 132). This work put the prophets in mind of the separation of the good and the wicked: so shall the divine winnower divide the chaff from the corn when He comes in judgement.

Exile and Return

In 587 B.C. Judah suffered the same fate as had overtaken Israel in 721: the destruction of its land and capital and the deportation of the ruling classes. The eloquent relief (Plate 122) serves thus to illustrate both calamities. The detail in Plate 133 shows the conquerors carrying objects from the city temple, a throne (for the divinity?) and a large jar for the public ceremonies, a striking illustration of what the Bible narrates concerning the stealing of the sacred jars (2 K 25.14; cf. Ezra 1.7). The significance of this robbery did not lie only in the material value of the objects taken. It meant above all that the god of the victors had conquered the god of the city. There are, however, radical differences in the material aspects of the two calamities. The attackers of 587 were the Chaldaeans under Nebuchadnezzar. In his numerous inscriptions this brilliant ruler never speaks of his military operations but only of his many expensive constructions for the benefit of gods and men – temples, towns, and irrigation works. If, however, Babylon provides but little information concerning the drama of Judah's fate, the Bible makes good the deficiency. Most details are supplied by Jeremiah's friend and biographer Baruch. They were supplemented in 1938 by the unexpected and moving testimony of the inscribed shards from Lachish (Plate 52, second from the left).

The fact that the Bible recounts Judah's fate in such detail is, however, closely bound up with the most important difference between 721 and 587: the exiles of Samaria were swallowed up in the Assyrian empire and disappeared without trace, those of Judah clung together and overcame as a group the effects of their

Plate 134. The Babylon of Nebuchadnezzar after a drawing by E. Unger based on the excavations. In the foreground is the bridge over the Euphrates; behind, the temple complex with the 'tower of Babel' (ground surface 90 by 90 metres – 295 by 295 ft); the famous processional route leads from here through the city.

Plate 133. Detail of Plate 122.

uprooting. The continued influence of Judah's more stable past and the leadership of men like Jeremiah and Ezekiel ensured that the destruction of the familiar background led only to an immeasurable strengthening of the ancient faith. In the fever of daily happenings the Judaeans had once scorned the prophets' warnings. What they had predicted had now come to pass. Thus their words bore weight and were indeed inspired by God and charged with power. But in that case this was also true of their promises concerning the 'remnant' who would return. The exiles zealously assembled all that remained of their prophecies, whether in the memory or already put down in writing. This was then read and commented upon as 'the Word of God', still operative in their time. Historical traditions too were carefully written down and edited. A new edition was made of the great chronicle of Josiah's time (see p. 85). Written as a national epic it could now be used in the national examination of conscience. The stirring poems of Deutero-Isaiah reveal the force of inspiration that could emanate from this reliving of the past. Elements of the magnificent Marduk liturgy in sacred Babylon, a city expanded by Nebuchadnezzar into the most brilliant metropolis of antiquity (Plate 134), were perhaps combined with purely Israelite data in this prophet's exposition of the treasures which the faith of Yahweh concealed. However this may be, during the year that followed Cyrus' rise to power (after 550) he fanned the smouldering fire of hope among the exiles and his profound vision of the perfect servant of God was couched in words in which, six centuries later, Jesus of Nazareth would see the expression of His Father's will. Less than a year after Cyrus had taken Marduk's city without a struggle he issued the famous edict which allowed

Plate 135. *Top*: coin from Judah, struck during the Persian domination but following the Attic model and bearing the owl of Athene. The three letters to the right are read as *J. H. D.*, the Aramaic form (Jehud) of the name Judah which occurs in the books of Ezra and Daniel. *Below*: silver spoon, 23 cm (9 in.) long, dated between 450 and 330 B.C., found in a tomb on the southern coastal plain. Spoons with handles consisting of a female body were very widespread in ancient Egypt; the elaboration of this idea, however, is here purely Syrian, as can be seen from the face of the woman, the two bulls' heads near the ring and the lotus motif between her hands.

the Judaeans to return to their country and to rebuild the temple at his cost. Then, in and around Jerusalem, laboriously, and under the watchful interest of the Persian kings, there came into being the 'post-Exilic community'. The foundations were laid by two princes of the house of David, Sheshbazzar and Zerubbabel, aided by Haggai and Zechariah. Fifty years later Ezra and Nehemiah returned from Persia with authority to adopt the measures which are recorded in their memoirs and which the Chronicler (see p. 85) combined with other documents in the books of Ezra and Nehemiah, to try to give a general account of the Return. With this the story ceases. We have practically no direct information concerning the period between 400 and 167 B.C. Archaeological data are also extremely rare (Plate 135). And yet, in these centuries, events occurred of immeasurable importance both for the writing of the Old Testament and for the later propagation of Christianity.

In learned priestly circles in Jerusalem the old story cycles of Yahwistic history (see p. 146) were supplemented by material of a later date and mostly ceremonious in character (e.g. Gn 1 and 17, Ex 25–31, 35–40, and Lv). Genealogical lists were added, ages and data serving as an ingenious chronology dating from the Creation (reckoned as 3761 B.C.). Thus in the fifth century there emerged 'the Law' (see p. 83) which had such a profound influence upon Jewish life and thought throughout the succeeding centuries. After this, earlier collections of prophetic writings were gathered into the present books, often supplemented by texts containing apocalyptic expectations (Is 24–7, Ezk 38–9), and new were added (Malachi, Obadiah, Jonah, Joel). The 'profane' proverbial 'wisdom' of earlier times (see p. 145) was practised in a

Plate 136. Persepolis, the magnificent court capital of Darius (521–485 B.C.) and Xerxes (485–464), where they received the yearly gifts of the tributary peoples and which was completely destroyed by Alexander the Great. Here, from Babylonian, Assyrian, Greek, and Egyptian motifs, the Persians developed their own style of architecture.

Plate 137. One of the delegations with gifts; detail from the reliefs which were exposed on the front of the palace terrace during the investigations of 1931–4. They are roughly 100 metres (330 ft) in length.

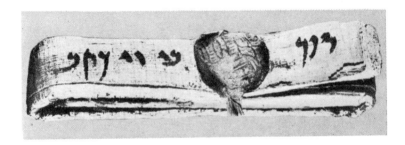

more explicitly religious manner (Pr 1–9 as introduction to the earlier collections 10–22 and 25–9). An exceptionally gifted writer composed the book of Job, and existing collections of psalms were augmented by new poems, mainly songs of praise and ingeniously turned didactic verses.

In the meantime, under the tolerant Persian princes who ruled either from Susa or from the glittering new capital of Persepolis (Plates 136–7), the 'Diaspora' began, the dispersion of the Jews throughout the empire (not always peaceable; see the book of Esther). The principal areas of this movement were Babylonia, where the largest section of Judaean exiles had remained behind, and Egypt, whither many had fled after the disaster of 587. Excavations on the island of Elephantine in the Nile opposite Assuân (Hebrew *Sewêne*, the Syene of Ezk 29.10, 30.6, the most southerly city of Egypt) revealed the existence of an important group of Jews, mainly soldiers in the service of Persia, in this economically and militarily important frontier city. The copies found there of letters and contracts (papyri of Elephantine, see Plates 138–9, a folded and sealed document and a few lines of writing underneath) throw light upon the relations of the distant imperial government with the Jewish cult even in this outpost, and upon the contacts of this colony with the centre in Jerusalem.

Plate 138. A folded and sealed contract from Elephantine on which can be read: *spr hî zî kth*, 'letter concerning a house, written by . . .'

Plate 139. The first lines of such a contract.

Plate 140. The Nile near Assuân, which is visible right, in the background. Elephantine is not the island in the foreground but the larger one behind it; on the photograph it is barely distinguishable from the city. Right, in the background, is the first cataract (counting from Cairo), where the Nile has to force its way through enormous blocks of granite. Here there are no fertile strips.

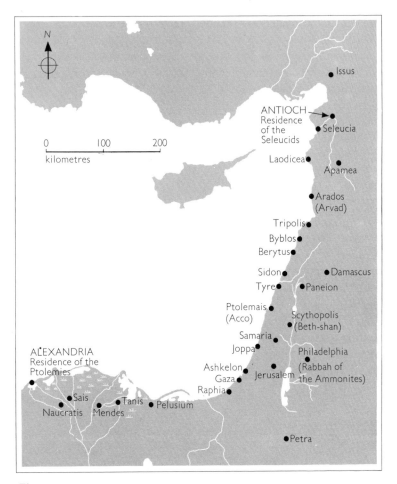

Figure 7

The Jews in the Hellenistic World

When, in 334 B.C., Alexander, who had set out at the age of twenty-two upon a retaliation expedition against the Persians, had broken the resistance of their naval base of Tyre (Plate 17), he pressed on into Egypt, which greeted him as a liberator. Inspired by his beloved poet Homer (*Od.* IV, 354), he founded the port of Alexandria opposite the island of Pharos (Plate 141). Then, strong in the conviction of his divine origin (Plate 143), the new Pharaoh set out for Mesopotamia. Darius III suffered a crushing defeat. Towards the end of 331 Persepolis (Plates 136–7) fell as sacrifice to the accumulated hate of many generations of Greeks. But Alexander wanted to go even farther, to the mighty sea that washes the shores of the world. When, four years later, in the strange land of India, his troops refused to advance farther eastwards, he had covered about 18,000 km (11,000 miles), fighting, conquering, and founding new cities after the Greek model. Back in Babylon after a wearying retreat, the thirty-three-year-old conqueror died (13 June 323), full of plans for the organization of his vast empire and for even more ambitious expeditions.

The Jewish community in Palestine was not directly affected by this young phenomenon. After the long-drawn-out wars among his successors, called the Diadochi, the coastal region fell, *c.* 300, to the Ptolemies, who ruled from Alexandria. The Seleucids, however, who afterwards had their capital at Antioch on the Orontes, claimed to be the lawful rulers. Palestine thus was the apple of discord between 'the kings of the north and the kings of the south' (see Dn 11, and Plates 144–5).

If at first the replacing of the Persian sovereigns by Greek

183

Plate 141. Alexandrian coin from the time of Commodus (A.D. 161–192), with the famous lighthouse on the island of Pharos, and a sailing ship.

Plate 142. A reconstruction drawing of the 180-metre-high (590-ft) construction, which was built under Ptolemy II Philadelphus (283–246 B.C.) and was considered one of the wonders of the world.

conquerors meant for the Jews of Jerusalem only a change of tax collectors, gradually their attitude towards the new culture became for them a matter of principle. Long before Alexander, elements of Greek civilization had penetrated deep into the Persian empire, borne there by merchants, mercenaries, and artists. For example, the coins struck *c.* 400 B.C. in the province of Judah, part of the Fifth Satrapy, followed the Attic model and

Plate 143. Alexander the Great shown as a god with the ram's horns, on a tetradrachm of *c.* 295 B.C.

Plates 144–5. Representatives of the two dynasties which fought for the possession of Palestine. 144: Ptolemy I (305–283); 145: Antiochus the Great (223–187).

Plate 146. For the Egyptian god Horus, whom the Ptolemies equated with the Greek Apollo, they built (in many stages, beginning in 237 B.C.) the magnificent temple at Edfu (100 km – 62½ miles – south of Luxor), which was then called Apollinopolis. Almost completely buried in Nile silt until the end of the last century, this temple is considered one of the best-preserved constructions of ancient times. It was erected according to the classical Egyptian model, but the details bear evidence of the strong influence of Greek culture.

Plate 147. Five coins. The upper specimen shows Antiochus IV Epiphanes (175–163 B.C.), who after his victory over Ptolemy VI in 169 began to call himself 'Theos Epiphanes', 'god made manifest in the flesh', and later added the title of Nikephoros, by which he in fact identified himself with Zeus. On the next coin he has had himself depicted with the wreath of victory and the beard of Zeus. The third coin shows Ptolemy III Euergetes, the deified 'benefactor' of his subjects, with the aureole of the sun god and the trident of Poseidon. Finally, the obverse and reverse of a Jewish coin of Alexander Jannaeus (Jannai was a childish form of Jonathan); the text in archaic letters reads: 'Jonathan high priest and the community of the Jews'. On other coins of his one reads on one side 'Jonathan the King' in Hebrew, and the other 'of King Alexander' in Greek.

Plate 148. Cleopatra; relief from the well-preserved Ptolemaic-Roman temple at Denderah (50 km – 31 miles – north of Luxor), dedicated to the goddess Hathor, who was identified with Aphrodite.

bore the image of Athene's owl (Plate 135). The new rulers, however, propagated the Hellenistic culture in a positive manner. Local gods were identified with Greek deities, and this was tolerated: the Syrian Baal-shamem, 'lord of the heavens', became Zeus, as did the Amon of Thebes in Egypt, where the talented Ptolemies revived the old culture (Plate 146). In Palestine the 'benefactors' (Plate 147) rebuilt old cities in the new style: Rabbah of the Ammonites became Philadelphia, Acco became Ptolemais. The educated people there spoke Greek, met in gymnasium and hippodrome, and were versed in the philosophy of the day.

But this way of life was difficult to reconcile with the precepts of the Law and Yahweh tolerated no identification with Zeus. Soon the Jewish community was split into two groups: the moderns, who wished to adapt the old faith to the new culture (these included many members of the upper and priestly classes), and the conservatives, who thought that their ancient heritage could only be preserved by a complete rejection of all Hellenistic influence (like the writer of the book Sirach or Ecclesiasticus, *c.* 190 B.C.). Between these two extremes were the doubters and sceptics (including perhaps the writer of Ecclesiastes), while in Egypt the old Hebraic books were translated into Greek. In 198 B.C. the great Antiochus III (Plate 145) brought Palestine finally under the dominion of the Seleucids. His son, Antiochus IV Epiphanes, who considered himself as an incarnation of Zeus (Plate 147, 1st and 2nd from the top), aroused the conservative party to revolt when he attempted to force them to adopt the Greek way of life and in 167 erected a statue of Zeus Olympius (perhaps made in his own likeness) in the temple of Jerusalem. The book of Daniel in its present form appeared during these years of crisis. The stories concerning this hero, assisted in so spectacular a fashion by the God of Israel in his revolt against pretentious rulers (Dn 1–6), were no less encouraging to the members of the resistance than the visions which were granted to him (Dn 7–12). These visions breathed the conviction that God had foreseen everything and was making ready to destroy utterly the fourth empire which, following upon those of the

Babylonians, Medes, and Persians, had dared to launch a direct attack upon Yahweh himself. After this He alone would rule in the nation of the saints represented by a mysterious figure 'like a Son of Man'.

In the first book of Maccabees, written *c.* 100 B.C. and surviving only in a Greek translation, one can find a reliable account of the revolt and actions of the leaders, Judas (166–160) and his brothers Jonathan (160–143) and Simon (142–134). This book also reveals how the movement, at the outset purely religious, was soon dominated by political aspirations.

Under the Roman Eagle

The great Antiochus III (223–187 B.C.), who had given asylum to Rome's arch-enemy, Hannibal, was crushingly defeated in 189 by Scipio Africanus in Asia Minor (near Magnesia, north-west of Smyrna). He was killed when he went to plunder old temples in Mesopotamia in order to be able to raise the heavy tributes exacted by Rome. His son Seleucus IV was under the same pressure and sent Heliodorus to Jerusalem to rob the Temple (2 Mac 3.7ff.; cf. Dn 11.20). His other son, Antiochus IV, had spent fourteen years as a hostage in Rome before being released in 176 B.C. He went to stay in the cultural centre of Athens, but left in 175 to seize the throne of his murdered brother Seleucus. He gained victories against the Ptolemies but when, in 168, he was on the point of annexing their kingdom to his own, he and all his troops were haughtily sent away from Egypt by the Roman consul Popilius Laenas. He departed to work off his rage on Jerusalem (cf. Dn 11.30).

The power of Rome prevailed at both ends of the coastal region, and it is thus understandable that the Maccabaean leaders should have turned to Rome for friendship and support in their struggle against the Seleucids. The author of the first book of Maccabees, who wrote his work in the classical Hebrew of Judges and Kings out of love for the great past which he thought now lived again, mentions these envoys to Italy with satisfaction. He evidently did not recall what – in that same great past – Isaiah thought of Hezekiah's embassies to Egypt for help against the

Plate 149. Roman soldiers with standards crossing a ship bridge; detail from the column of Trajan in Rome.

Assyrians (Is 30, 31). Devoted to the dynasty of the Hasmonaeans (as the successors of the Maccabees are usually called, in imitation of Josephus), he sees in them the revival of the old kingship (cf. the closing sentence of his book with 1 K 14.29). Their rule, however, reposed upon a different and too narrow basis. For the Maccabaean brothers were supported by only a section of the people, the devout, who followed the Law. The higher classes and many priestly families adopted the new culture and accepted the Seleucid rulers (cf. p. 188). When we read (in Josephus) that John Hyrcanus (135–104) undertook successful campaigns in Transjordan and against Samaria and that he forced the Idumaeans in the south to adopt the Jewish religion and circumcision, we must not think of campaigns like those of David and Josiah. John's army consisted mainly of pagan mercenaries and their leader behaved almost like a pagan ruler. Those who still were faithful to the Law rejected him, and some went off to live near the Dead Sea (cf. p. 199). During this time arose the party of the Pharisees, strongly opposed to the Sadducees, members of the old priestly families who, from the time of Jonathan Maccabaeus, had rebelled against the fact that he and his successors had assumed the office of High Priest.

Aristobulus (104–103), who murdered some of his blood relations and forced Judaism upon the Ituraeans in the north, was

Plate 150. Three tomb monuments at the entrance to the narrow cleft in the rocks which gives access to Petra. They were made by cutting away the surrounding rock. The monument on the left (note the small figure) appears to be an imitation of an altar.

Plate 151. One of the countless tombs hewn out of the rose-red rock walls surrounding the city.

Plate 152. An aerial photograph of the west side of Petra; the small rock in the centre bore the acropolis of this immensely wealthy trading city, which extended into the valley on the left and knew its greatest period of prosperity during the first century of our era (King Aretas IV even ruled Damascus; see 2 Co 11.32). The enormous, steep rock which can be seen above the acropolis, and whose top lies 200 metres (656 ft) higher than the city, is considered to be the site of the Edomite capital of Sela (the name means 'rock', as does Petra), which was conquered by Amaziah (2 K 14.7, 2 Ch 25.12).

succeeded by his brother Alexander Jannaeus (103–76; see Plate 147, foot), who conquered nearly the whole of Palestine and the Transjordan. But he used his pagan mercenaries against his own people and made himself especially hated among the Pharisees. His widow, Alexandra (76–67), restored their influence in the government and appointed her feeble son Hyrcanus High Priest. After her death the latter came into conflict with his energetic younger brother Aristobulus, who had the support of the malcontents, notably the Sadducees and the army commanders. On the advice of Antipater, the father of Herod the Great, Hyrcanus sought the support of the Nabataeans, who began to exercise considerable power from their capital Petra (Plates 150–52). Aristobulus, with the Sadducees and the pagan mercenaries, was engaged in fighting against his brother Hyrcanus, with his Pharisees and the Nabataean army, when word came that the Roman commander Pompey had arrived in Syria to annex what remained of the Seleucid empire for Rome (64 B.C.). What followed then was significant. Among the envoys who paid their respects to Pompey were three from Judaea: one from the energetic Aristobulus and his Sadducees with a request for intervention; one under the guidance of Antipater to ask help for Hyrcanus and the Pharisees; and one from the common people begging the Roman to put an end to the rule of the Hasmonaeans. This scene is significant in showing the rapid decay of the Maccabaean house and also characterizes the decades that followed: anyone wishing to gain or retain power in Judaea must first obtain the favour of Rome.

Pompey recognized Hyrcanus as High Priest (63–40) but drastically curtailed his power. In 40 the Parthians, Rome's strongest enemy in the east, invaded Syria and Palestine, deposed Hyrcanus and replaced him by Antigonus (40–37), the son of his old enemy Aristobulus. Herod, who had previously shown himself as crafty in intrigue as his father Antipater, then went to Rome, convinced Antony and Octavian of his rights, and was made king of Judaea in 40 B.C. He had, however, to conquer his

Plate 153. Corner of the great temple square at Palmyra (see Plate 154), showing that the influence of Greek taste reached far into the Syrian desert. Left, the monumental entrance gate to the city beyond it, an Arabian fort.

kingdom himself. After a subject visit to Antony, who in the meantime had left for Syria to repel the Parthians, he obtained Roman troops and with them took Judaea and Jerusalem, where he had all his enemies put to death. At the outset of his reign (37 B.C.) Herod had to employ all his diplomatic talents to retain the confidence of the triumphant Antony on the one hand, and on the other to resist the intrigues of the latter's mistress Cleopatra (Plate 148), who was trying to obtain Syria and Palestine as the Pharaohs of antiquity and the first Ptolemies had done. After Antony's defeat at Actium (31 B.C.) Herod quickly changed sides and offered his allegiance and help to the victor Octavian, who in 27 was granted the title *Augustus*, that is 'exalted', 'divine', *Sebastos* in Greek, the language spoken by cultured people in Rome. For the Romans were strongly Hellenized, and it is certain that the many edifices built by Herod in honour of his imperial benefactor (cf. p. 213) were in the Greek style, like the later temples of Palmyra (Plates 153–4) and Ba'albek (Plate 155), which give us some idea of Herod's buildings. By systematically putting to death every person who could possibly be regarded as a pretender to the throne Herod tried to make his position secure, and by visits to Rome he strengthened his relations with the most powerful man in the world.

Plate 154. An aerial photograph of Palmyra, the trading city in the desert which flourished in the second century A.D., replacing Petra in importance. The temple in the foreground (the sides are 225 metres (738 ft) long; in 1935 a whole village was removed from it!) was begun when Jesus was a boy. Above the sanctuary in the centre can be seen the corner which is shown in close-up in Plate 153; behind it is the monumental gate to the central arcade.

Plate 155. The famous temple complex at Ba'albek, dedicated to the Baal of the Beqa', who, after the time of Alexander, was identified with Helios the sun god and venerated by the Romans as Jupiter Heliopolitanus. In his honour they built in the second century A.D. the structure which has suffered much from attacks and earthquakes and in which a Christian church and an Arabian fort were built. On the plate can be seen, to the right, one of the restored exedrae in the arcade which surrounded the great forecourt (120 metres by 100 metres –394 by 328 ft); left, behind the gully which contained the foundations of the church, which has now been pulled down, can be seen an altar and then the mighty entrance stairway to the temple of Jupiter, 7·5 metres (24 ft) higher. Of its 54 pillars, 20 metres (66 ft) high and 2·2 metres (7 ft) in diameter, only six remain.

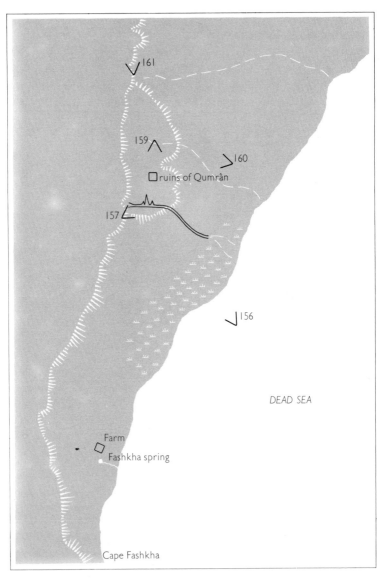

Figure 8

Voices in the Wilderness

During the turbulent years of the revolt of the Maccabees another group had emerged alongside those of the Pharisees and Sadducees, that of the Essenes. Flavius Josephus (*c*. A.D. 37–100), the Jewish historian who spent fully thirty-five years of his life in Palestine and whose works are our most important source of information concerning the history of the Jews after the Maccabaean rising, speaks of them as already existing at the time of Jonathan (160–143). Probably as a reaction against the corruption in Jerusalem, these devout people sought above all outward and inward purity. They held all their goods in common and lived in poverty and in obedience to a superior chosen by themselves. They refrained from commerce and took no part in the bloody animal sacrifices, although they rigorously followed the Law of Moses. Remarkable for their white clothing, their peculiar practices (e.g. morning prayers facing the rising sun) and some not entirely Jewish doctrines, they are mentioned by the Alexandrian Jew Philo (*c*. 25 B.C.–A.D. 50) and by the pagan Pliny (*c*. A.D. 23–79). The latter confirms their connection with the Dead Sea and adds that they dwelt a little distance from the shore on account of the evil mists which rose from the sea. Since they are not mentioned in the New Testament or in any of the official Jewish records, they were neglected until recently, except for a few specialists in Jewish history. This suddenly changed in 1949 when it was revealed that scrolls had been found two years before in a cave near the Dead Sea. There is now no magazine that has not devoted an article to the story of the remarkable finds: the shepherd boy throwing stones through a gap in the rock wall and,

hearing a metallic sound, creeping through the hole and finding jars with written scrolls inside them; the further investigations in other caves and the excavation of the only visible remains of human habitation, the ruin of *Qumrân*. Yet although the details are now well known these publications usually devote little attention to the setting in which all this took place. The photographs here seek to illustrate this background. They can be studied with the aid of Figure 8, upon which their areas are indicated. In Plate 156, taken from an aeroplane above the Dead Sea looking north-west, one sees the water (black) to the right and to the left the mountain wall with the plateau transected by the winter rains from the mountain range. The ruin of *Qumrân* stands upon the area above the rugged north side of this incision.

In Plate 157, taken from the edge of the mountain facing north-east (the water of the Dead Sea is here white), the rectangular ruin on the plateau is seen as a black patch. Above it are some of the diggers' tents, with two more tents to the right. An indentation can be seen on the foremost spur: this is the enlarged entrance to cave No. 4. The photographer of Plate 158 stood near the tent above it, to the right, thus having cave No. 4 in the foreground (note the camel grazing far below to the left!) and in the background the mountain wall from which he took Plate 157. This spot can be found in the foreground of the aerial photograph, Plate 159, which looks towards the south. From a point between the plateau and the shore of the Dead Sea (see Plate 156) the panorama of Plate 160 stretches westwards: left, the plateau, behind it, and running its whole length, the rugged reddish-brown rock face. In Plate 161 a man points to the original opening, the small hole through which the Bedouin boy threw his stones, with such interesting results.

On investigating the ruin (Plate 162, looking south-east), it was discovered that building began under Hyrcanus (135–104). The complex was destroyed, either by the Parthians in 40 B.C. (see p. 195) or by the earthquake of 31 B.C. (see the large crack in one of

Plate 156. An aerial view of the plateau of *Qumrân*.

Plate 157. The plateau seen from the high rock wall; in the background is the northern part of the Dead Sea.

Plate 158. The spur in which cave No. 4 is situated.

Plate 159. An aerial photograph in a southerly direction; the rectangular ruin is clearly visible in the foreground; behind slopes the fantastic wâdi wall which, together with the steep mountain wall to the right, forms the background of Plate 158. Upper right, the fantastic relief of the desert of Judaea.

Plate 160. The rock wall and the plateau seen from near the shore of the Dead Sea.

Plate 161. The position of cave No. 1.

Plate 164. The refectory of the fraternity.

Plate 162. The ruin on the plateau; to the right is the spur from which Plate 158 was taken, looking towards cave No. 4.

Plate 163. The steps of one of the many cisterns; the left half has subsided as the result of an earthquake.

Plate 165. The examination of a cave; the soil is carefully scraped away and then carried outside in baskets.

Plate 166. Most of the documents were found in small fragments; cave No. 4 alone yielded thousands, from hundreds of different manuscripts.

Plate 167. With infinite patience an international team of scholars in the Rockefeller Museum sorts and studies the fragments. A small selection, carefully held together between glass plates, is spread out on the tables.

the cisterns: Plate 163), and remained a ruin until the beginning of our era. It was then restored and flourished until its final destruction by the Romans in A.D. 68.

The complex, with its large rooms (see Plate 164), was not a dwelling house. The people who used it apparently lived in caves and tents, and met there to eat and pray together and to copy their sacred books (Plates 55–6) while supporting themselves by the work of their hands. In 1958 outbuildings came to light near the *Fashkha* spring (see Figure 8), a sort of farm with workshops in which the inhabitants of *Qumrân* dried dates (the salt marsh, black on Plate 159, is very suitable for date palms), cured the hides of their cattle, and so on. A laborious investigation of the whole length of the rock wall (Plate 165) showed that ten other caves possessed the remains of manuscripts, most of them in a very fragmentary state (Plates 166–7).

Thus, thanks to the curiosity of a shepherd boy and the energetic intervention of professional archaeologists of many different nationalities, we have gained insight into the manner of life and thought of a group of Jesus' contemporaries, identical or very closely related to the Essenes of Josephus and Philo. The remains of their careful copies of the Biblical books are of inestimable value for our knowledge of the textual history of the Old Testament. Possibly even more important are their Biblical commentaries and their own writings, which show how these Jewish contemporaries of Jesus, far from the bustle of the town, found a new interpretation of the ancient piety of the Pharisees and lived in tense expectation of the absolute rule of God that was soon to come.

Plate 168. Young shepherd wearing a head-cloth, followed by his sheep.

The Hireling and the Good Shepherd

Pagan contemporaries called King Herod (37–4 B.C.) 'the Great'. He was undoubtedly a capable ruler and promoted agriculture, trade, and industry. With keen insight he had one of the few anchorages on the coast enlarged to form the excellent port of Sebastos, and built a completely new town, Caesarea, the 'imperial', which was soon to become the real capital of Judah. He adorned the large hill of Samaria (Plate 120) with a magnificent city which, again out of gratitude to Augustus (see p. 197), came to be called Sebaste. At its highest point a temple was built in honour of the emperor (Plate 169). Outside Palestine, in Tyre, Damascus, Antioch, Rhodes, and even Athens he built temples, porticoes, and colonnades.

He was, however, hated by his subjects, partly on account of the heavy taxes he imposed to pay for all this magnificent display, but especially by those who lived by the old traditions. To begin with, Herod was not a real Jew, but a descendant of the ancient Edomites whose name had become almost synonymous with 'arch-enemy of God'. If David of Judah was once taken from his flocks in order to care for God's people and to rule them in the name of God, the prototype of the good shepherd (Ezk 34.16), this intruder, Herod, ruled in the name of the Romans who had given him his power. He was only able to maintain his authority

Plate 169. The only remaining part of Herod's temple in Samaria, built in honour of Augustus; the entrance stairway.

Plates 170–71. 170: the tomb of Abraham at Hebron with the magnificent ring wall of Herod, which is seen in close-up in Plate 171.

with the help of Roman mercenaries, an uncircumcised rabble from all the countries of the world. Scarcely had he ascended the throne when he audaciously took control of the office of High Priest, to which he appointed unworthy candidates whom he deposed and murdered whenever it suited his ruthless policy.

In order to gain the favour of his pious subjects Herod not only built a magnificent enclosing wall about the highly venerated burial cave of Abraham near Hebron (Plates 170–71) but began a grandiose restoration and extension of the Temple in Jerusalem. He expanded the building surface into the enormous terrace which even now compels admiration (Plate 183). One must imagine it covered with a shining white main building whose roof was overlaid with gold leaf, and surrounded by grandiose colonnades. But higher than the temple terrace, and built before it was, stood a fortress, the Antonia, called after Herod's former Roman friend, and higher still, in the upper quarters of the town, was his palace with its three famous towers. For the King, by nature suspicious and jealous, knew that he was hated, and built himself fortresses even outside Jerusalem. He restored some of the mountain fortresses of the Hasmonaeans, preferably in the inaccessible region around the Dead Sea. Among these were Masada, Machaerus (Plate 27), and Hyrcanium (Plate 28). He also built new citadels, such as the Herodium south-east of Bethlehem (Plate 179), where he was buried.

At this time Jesus was already born. The pilgrim who visits Bethlehem for the sake of Him, the Good Shepherd, looks down over the little town upon the abandoned tomb of Herod the Great – the wicked hireling (Plate 29).

The Gospels: Background and Composition

Figure 9 (pp. 216–17) is intended to do two things: to give a simplified survey of the complex political history which forms the background of the Gospels and of the Acts, and to form the basis for a short discussion on the special character of these chronicles. At the extreme left of the plan are the Roman emperors in capital letters, for their will ruled the world of politics. The names in smaller print found between them are some of the legates who governed Syria in their name and also kept watch on the course of events in Palestine. The list in the middle is headed by Herod the Great.

After Herod's death in 4 B.C. Augustus divided his territory among three of his sons whom he had not murdered: Archelaus, Herod Antipas, and Philip. The first ruled Judaea and Samaria as ethnarch ('ruler of the people', less than 'king', but the ordinary man made no distinction; Mt 2.22). He ruled badly (cf. Lk 19.12, 14) and was banished in A.D. 6. His territory then fell under governors, procurators, and the supervision of the legates in Syria. Herod Antipas ruled as tetrarch ('ruler of a fourth part', a worn-out title for rulers of small areas) much longer than his brother. Having come under suspicion in Rome he was banished to Lyon in A.D. 39. Philip, the best of the three, died childless in 34. His tetrarchy first came under Syria, but one of Herod's grandsons, Agrippa, educated in Rome, by playing his cards cleverly, was successful in obtaining it from Caligula, who also gave him Antipas' region in A.D. 39. In 41 he received Judaea and Samaria from his friend the emperor Claudius, so that from 41 to 44 he ruled as king over all the lands of his grandfather. One of his brothers, Herod, was made king of Chalcis, in the Beqa' (see

Emperors	Judaea/Samaria governors	Herod's sons	Years	Events
AUGUSTUS	HEROD THE GREAT — Ruler of Palestine 39–4 B.C. Augustus divided this region among Herod's three sons			
Quintilius Varus	ARCHELAUS (Judaea and Samaria)	HEROD ANTIPAS (Galilee and Peraea)	PHILIP (Ituraea, Trachonitis, etc.)	Birth of Jesus 6 B.C.
			10	
Volusius Saturninus				
Quirinius	Caponius 6–9		1	
	M. Ambibulus 9–12			
TIBERIUS	Annius Rufus 12–15		10	
	Valerius Gratus 15–26			
			20	John the Baptist. Preaching of Jesus
	Pontius Pilate 26–36		30	Passion and Death of Jesus. Community of Jerusalem. Death of Stephen. Paul becomes a Christian
Vitellius	Marcellus 36–37			
CALIGULA	Marullus 37–41	granted to Agrippa I	granted to Agrippa I	Community in Antioch. James beheaded, Peter taken prisoner
Petronius			40	
CLAUDIUS	AGRIPPA I 41–44			
		Herod of Chalcis		

Assembly in Jerusalem

Paul's second journey
1 Th 2 Th

Paul's third journey
*Ph? 1 Co Gal
Ro 2 Co*

Paul captured in
Caesarea, taken to
Rome
*Col Philem Eph
1 Ti 1 Tit
Mk 2 Ti*

Martyrdom of Peter
and Paul
*Mt?
Lk-Ac?*

*Rev 2 and 3 Ep of Jn?
Jn 1 Ep of Jn*

| 50 |
| 60 |
| 70 |
| 80 |
| 90 |
| 100 |

Agrippa II
of Chalcis

Agrippa II
Trachonitis, etc.

Agrippa II

...tus Alexander 46-48

Ventidius Cumanus 48-52

Antonius Felix 52-60

Porcius Festus 60-62

Albinus 62-64

Gessius Florus 64-66

Jewish uprising

Jerusalem destroyed
by Titus

Judaea an imperial
province, legates

Josephus writes
History of the Jewish War

Josephus writes
Jewish Antiquities

Cassius Longinus

Ummidius Quadratus

NERO

Corbulo

Cestius Gallus

Mucianus

GALBA etc.
VESPASIAN

TITUS

DOMITIAN

NERVA
TRAJAN

Figure 9

p. 19). On his terrible death, his son, Agrippa II, was too young to succeed him and Claudius appointed procurators to govern the greater part of his kingdom. Once again they formed a series of seven. In 48 Agrippa II was allowed to succeed his uncle in Chalcis and in 53 Claudius made him king of the regions formerly ruled by Philip and Lysanias (cf. Lk 3.1). Nero granted him a few more pieces of Galilee and Peraea in A.D. 64. This extremely Roman-minded king appears to have ruled until after A.D. 90. He was appointed inspector of the Jewish cult in Jerusalem. In 66 he tried to stop the senseless revolt but it continued to spread and led to the terrible destruction of Jerusalem in the year 70.

After this Judaea was governed by Roman legates. The holy city was rebuilt in the Roman style and no Jew was allowed to enter it. This was a great blow to Jews and Christians everywhere, but for the Christians this calamity had also a positive meaning. It confirmed their conviction that the history of Israel, meant as a preparation for God's universal dominion over all nations, was now at an end and that the lasting kingdom of God had really arrived. This conviction had lodged in the hearts of those who, forty years before, had been taught by Jesus of Nazareth and had seen him alive after His crucifixion and burial, and they had spread it throughout the empire, even in Rome itself. There, two of their leaders, Peter and Paul, had already paid with their lives for worshipping Jesus as the Messiah and the only true Lord of mankind.

The right-hand side of Figure 9 shows how matters stood around A.D. 70. Most of the letters of the New Testament have already been written and also the Gospel of St Mark. The Gospels of St Matthew and St Luke are accompanied by a query, since it is not certain whether they were written before or after A.D. 70. At the bottom of the list stands the Gospel of St John, written towards the end of the century.

These four documents are called in Greek *evangelion*, meaning 'glad tidings'; they grew out of the proclamation of Christ's teaching. The first preaching in Jerusalem concerned the resurrection of Jesus: 'This man Jesus, whom you crucified (this you

Plate 172. The village of *Kafr Kenna*.

all know well) was raised by God from the dead and is thus the Messiah, appointed Lord and Judge of all . . .' For those not fully acquainted with the arrest and execution a sober account was given here which naturally, among the first preachers, scarcely differed. The same is true of the Bible texts chosen to elucidate the meaning of the Passion of the Messiah and of His Resurrection.

The case was slightly different when they came to write down what they remembered of their contact with Jesus, of His words, His miracles, His sermons, and His parables. Each witness drew upon his store of memories in his own manner (everyone remembers experiences in a different way) and put them into words whenever they were called upon to describe Jesus as a man or tell of His mission. Naturally, in the course of much preaching and instruction of assistants these memories gradually assumed a more definite form and were written down. It is probable that as early as the fifth decade several of these collections were circulating in the then bilingual early Church, written both in Aramaic (including one by St Matthew, according to an early tradition) and in Greek. With the aid of such material Mark, the Greek adapter of Matthew, and Luke wrote the three Gospels named after them, remaining faithful to their sources yet retaining their own individuality as writers.

This process of composition had two main consequences. Since the Gospels (including the fourth, that of St John) are based upon a richly varied series of personal recollections, they give a more concrete picture of Jesus and of the impression He made upon His contemporaries than any critical biography in the modern manner could ever have done. Furthermore, since these reminiscences were formulated in order to further the proclamation of Jesus as the Messiah and Saviour of mankind they do not record such details as 'where' exactly, or 'when', often not even 'how'. Each Evangelist, although conscious of writing history,

Plate 173. Bethlehem.

Plate 174. Shepherds in the so-called 'field of the shepherds' near Bethlehem, which can just be seen in the background.

handles his material in his own way and with a freedom which nowadays amazes us.

The ways in which this method of composition affects our knowledge of Jesus' public life are discussed in the next chapter. First let us contemplate the photograph (Plate 172) of an Arabic village. It gives an excellent idea of the surroundings in which Jesus lived and worked until, a man of thirty, He entered upon the public scene.

Jesus of Nazareth

Plate 175 shows a section of present-day Nazareth, looking south. In the background is the plain of Jezreel. Here Jesus will undoubtedly have stood as a boy gazing out over the wide plain with its historic memories, towards the Carmel ridge farther west, a reminder to every Jew of Elijah the fiery warrior of God, eastwards to the mountains of Gilboa (Plate 94), celebrated by David in a song which every Jew knew by heart, and still farther east towards majestic Mount Tabor, which will have reminded Him of Barak's fight for the God of Israel (Plate 88). What lay directly before Him, however, was very different from what appears on the photo. Nazareth was then no busy pilgrimage centre, but an insignificant little village, mentioned neither by the Old Testament, nor by Josephus, nor by the Jewish Talmud. Other villages in Galilee (Plates 172 and 176) give a better idea of what it must have been like than Nazareth itself. There Jesus assisted His father in the carpenter's shop which He later took over. The simple people among whom He lived are brilliantly sketched in his parables, of which it has rightly been said that no other literature of Roman imperial times gives such a lively picture of the daily life of the common people.

The nature of Jesus' inner life is strikingly indicated by St Luke, who records Him, a twelve-year-old who has remained behind in the temple during a pilgrimage to Jerusalem, as saying to His parents: 'Did you not know that I must be about My Father's business?' (Luke 2.49).

When he was about thirty years old John's call to conversion and repentance reached Nazareth. Jesus heard it and left His

Plate 175. Present-day Nazareth; in the background can be seen the plain of Jezreel, whose name was corrupted in Christian times to Esdraelon.

family in order to be baptized in the winding Jordan (Plates 177–8). It is no longer possible to determine exactly where this baptism took place: a Bethany 'beyond the Jordan' (Jn 1.28) is not mentioned anywhere else, and the place Aenon (the name means roughly 'regions of springs'), where John baptized 'because there was much water there' and which lay near Salim (Jn 3.23), is also impossible to locate with certainty.

After a sojourn in the barren wilderness of Judaea (Plate 179), since that time a favourite region for Christian anchorites (Plates 21–2), Jesus proceeded to Galilee. There He began to preach that the kingdom of God was at hand, continuing in His own way the task of John the Baptist, who at this time lay imprisoned in the

Plate 176. Village in Galilee.

Plate 177. One of the many bends of the Jordan.

224

Plate 178. The Jordan near Jericho; in the background are the fantastic marl hills which flank the river bed (see Plate 3).

fortress of Machaerus east of the Dead Sea (Plate 27), as punishment for his outspokenness to Herod Antipas. Jesus preached mainly in the region around the Sea of Galilee (Plate 180), shown on this photo from the west. In the foreground, on the coast with its delightful climate and medicinal warm springs, lies Tiberias, the city founded between A.D. 17 and 22 by Herod Antipas to be the new capital of his tetrarchy and named after his overlord in

Plate 179. Part of the wilderness of Judaea; in the foreground are the enclosures of stones in which the shepherds gather their sheep at night; the dark patches are cultivated land. Above the centre is the cone-shaped ruin of the Herodium, the fortress which Herod built and destined to be his tomb. Above it are the little houses of the village of *Beit Sahûr* and to the left is Bethlehem.

Plate 180 (*following pages*). Tiberias on the Sea of Galilee; the inhabitants of the other shore had more contact with those on this side than with the people of the barely accessible highland behind them.

Plate 181. A man draws water from a cistern for a woman who will carry the filled jars on her head back to her tent.

Rome, Tiberius. In common with other devout Jews of this region, Jesus appears to have avoided this city, which had adopted Hellenistic morals and manners. He was most at home (in so far as this phrase can be used in connection with Him) in Capernaum, about 10 km (6 miles) farther north, now, apart from the synagogue, a heap of ruins like Chorazin, and, on the northeast shore, Beth-saida. This town belonged to the tetrarchy of Philip and was rebuilt by him at the beginning of our era and named Julias, in honour of a daughter of Augustus.

Plate 182. A farmer ploughing his land, a thin layer of soil strewn with stones, on a foundation of rock.

Plate 183. The temple square in Jerusalem.

In Capernaum lived Peter, Andrew, and the sons of Zebedee, the first disciples, who at a word from Jesus abandoned their little fishing businesses in order to follow Him, such was the strength of His fascination for them. For the coming reign of God, seen by John the Baptist as judgement, sentence, and the destruction of the wicked, was characterized by Jesus as the revelation of the merciful love of God, whom, in an incomparable way, He called His Father. Still more, He spoke of this revelation as having already begun in his own person and confirmed this by limiting Satan's domain wherever He thought good: He drove out devils, healed the sick, and even raised the dead to life. For, wherever the living God is obeyed completely and rules absolutely, sickness and death lose their power. Although we know little of the sequence and routes of Jesus' journeys, His stay in the distant regions of Tyre and Sidon appears to coincide with a crisis in His Ministry. After Peter's profession of faith in the country of Caesarea Philippi and the Transfiguration on the Mount (nearby Mount Hermon? or Mount Tabor?), He began to prepare His disciples for the suffering He would have to undergo in Jerusalem and which would definitely ratify the revelation of God's kingship.

Before this time Jesus had journeyed to Jerusalem for the great feasts only, time and again to come up against the lack of comprehension of the leading circles, as in the mysterious district of Dalmanutha-Magadan. Sometimes in the course of these journeys He passed through Samaria, where, at the well of Jacob near Shechem (Plate 66), He once spoke with a woman drawing water (see Plate 181), and sometimes through the eastern part of the Jordan valley, which formed part of Peraea. The frontiers of the various territories given on Map 9 obviously did not prevent

Plate 184. The Kidron valley with the corner of the temple square which is partly visible in Plate 183. The sepulchral monument in the centre probably existed in the time of Christ; the Jewish tombs are of a much later date.

Plate 185. A street in Jerusalem.

Plate 186. A street which descends from the upper town to the old hill of Zion, a street where Jesus may have walked.

Plate 187. The usual disposition of the Jewish graves around Jerusalem in the time of Herod. An open passage (1) was hewn in the slope of a hill, usually with a few steps in order to attain the required depth more quickly. Behind a very low opening, which could be sealed by rolling a stone in front of it, a room was dug out (2), with benches against the walls (2a), and then a second room (3), with one or more niches in the walls in which the dead were placed (3a). The floor of the niche often sloped slightly so that the fluid produced by decomposition could run off into a hole. After a time only the skeleton remained, and it was collected when the niche was required for another body and buried either in a small opening in the floor or in a small chest (ossuarium).

Plate 188. The entrance to a tomb near Jerusalem, with a stone.

Plate 189. Perfume jars and lamps from a tomb on the Mount of Olives dating from the time of Christ.

Plate 190. An inscription on an ossuarium found there; it reads 'Martha and Mary'.

234

freedom of movement. His last journey also lay through Peraea, to the city which enjoyed the lugubrious fame of being fatal to prophets. There He boldly appeared in the temple (Plate 183), which was still being built, and openly prophesied its destruction. In the evenings He walked through the deep valley of the Kidron (Plate 184) or to His friends in Bethany or to the Garden of Gethsemane at the foot of the Mount of Olives. For the site of these and other places from the story of the Passion, see the map of Jerusalem (Map 5), to be compared with the aerial photographs (Plates 104–6). The site of the Pavement or Gabbatha (see Plate 183) is extremely doubtful and consequently the route of Jesus' wearying Way of the Cross through narrow and often stepped streets (Plate 186). We know for certain, however, where Calvary stood. This rise in the ground, commonly called Golgotha, 'skull', lay in Jesus' time just outside the city gate where many roads met. Nowadays this piece of rock and the tomb a little farther up, hewn out in a garden (Plates 187–8), are covered by a not very beautiful complex of churches, the first goal of every Christian on arrival in Jerusalem. For the Pharisees the Jesus affair was definitely closed on that Friday: had God been with this man He would certainly have saved him from death.

'My Witnesses to the End of the Earth'

To Luke, a doctor from Antioch (Plate 196) who became Paul's most faithful companion, we owe not only the third Gospel, with its particularly sensitive portrait of the Saviour, but also that document which we know as the 'Acts of the Apostles' and which the author intended as a sequel to his Gospel. Some find it advisable to begin the reading of the New Testament with this book. The first chapters indeed give a stirring picture of the overwhelming impression which Jesus' resurrection made upon His disciples, transforming them from vacillating and fearful followers into courageous witnesses who knew themselves to be supported by an all-conquering power.

The various speeches of Peter recorded by Luke are so archaic in style and content that he must either have employed written sources or have been able to enter completely into the transports of the first days and months. However this may be, it is extremely profitable to compare these accounts of the first preaching (see Ac 2, 3, 4 and 10; cf. 13) and to see for oneself how, relying on Old Testament texts, the disciples saw Jesus' resurrection as the seal of God upon His Ministry and how they considered these facts decisive for the whole of humanity and for every man, being the commencement of the long-awaited kingdom of God. Taking this into account one becomes more easily reconciled to the fact that the Gospel stories concerning Jesus' resurrection and apparitions are so disconnected and on some points cannot even be reconciled with each other. Each evangelist obviously drew upon the traditions at his disposal and it is understandable that the recollections of the marvellous experiences of those days of profound emotion

should have differed so strongly. The important fact is that all the people who first recounted and transmitted these stories belonged to the communities which we see springing up in the Acts: the link which bound these people together (and also painfully divided them from the Jewish community) was the conviction that God had raised his servant Jesus from the dead and, having raised him to his right hand, had appointed him Lord and Messiah, the Saviour of all mankind. They had either seen Him alive themselves or placed their trust in the testimony of those to whom He had appeared and to whom He had given His world-embracing commission.

Luke devotes the second and larger part of his work to Paul. It is significant that this thoughtful writer, who is usually careful to avoid repetition, includes three detailed accounts of Paul's experience on the road to Damascus (in Ac 9, 22, and 26). This is evidently his way of expressing the immeasurable importance of this event for the young Christian church. Seldom, indeed, was anyone better equipped than Paul for the task that awaited him. Born at Tarsus in Cilicia of orthodox Jewish parents, and sent to Jerusalem as a child to receive legal training as a Rabbi from masters who included the famous Gamaliel, he was familiar with the two main forms of Jewish life, of the Dispersion and of Jerusalem. By his command of 'Koinè' Greek, spoken by cultured people of these times, he was able to communicate with all the educated people of the empire. He had inherited Roman citizenship, a privilege that included all kinds of facilities and which even high-ranking officers were sometimes obliged to purchase at a considerable price. He was capable of quick and clear reasoning and elevated mystical contemplation. He had, in addition, an extremely agile mind, capable of experiencing a whole range of feeling within a few seconds. Paul had, from his youth, placed all these gifts at the service of his God. Even more than his colleagues he detested the followers of Jesus, for he saw more clearly than they that this sect threatened the very foundations of the Jewish community, the heritage of God. He continued to hold

Plate 191. The Cilician Gates, one of the passes through the Taurus mountains, which St Paul frequently crossed with great danger.

this view until, near Damascus, it was made clear to him that in combating the supporters of Jesus he was fighting, not the enemies of his God, but the Messiah, the Christ for whom he had longed from his youth. If one reads Paul's letters in the light of the journeys which Luke records and in the order of their writing (Map 10 may be of help here) one sees how during this restless coming and going, through desolate mountain passes (Plate 191), in battered little ships, and along endless roads (Plate 193), he penetrates deeper into the reality which is finally revealed to him upon the road to Damascus and in the Street called Straight (Plate 194).

It was not only the will to convey his message plainly and convincingly in the most diverse circles, among Jews and heathens, educated and illiterate, which impelled him to ceaseless reflection, but also the crises and defections of some of his community. The faithful of Thessalonica lead him to clarify the doctrine of the second coming of Jesus (who had died barely twenty years before) and the Jewish teachers in Galatia lead him to define more clearly the doctrine of justification by faith. The converts of the turbulent metropolis of Corinth (Plate 195), with their questions and disputes, draw from him some sublime pages, and during his two years' imprisonment in Rome the fallacies of the Colossians lead him to a consideration of the final consequences of Jesus' work for humanity and for the universe. Luke's work ends with the mention of this stay in Rome (61–63). Paul made other journeys after this, to judge from his letters to Timothy and Titus, in which he draws up measures for the

Plate 192. The arrival of a Roman trading ship, probably in the port of Ostia; the captain offers sacrifice on the rear deck in thanksgiving for a safe return. To the right of the ship stands Neptune; other statues stand in various places in the harbour. On the base of one of them is depicted a chariot drawn by four elephants; the rider is perhaps the emperor Claudius, the founder of the harbour. This relief contains many interesting details: the structure of the ship, the rigging, the sails, the sloops, etc. St Paul travelled in ships like these. Relief, 3rd century A.D., *Museo Torlonia, Rome*.

Plate 193. Roman milestone beside an ancient highway that leads over the fertile highland from Dibon to Medeba (*Madaba*), visible in the distance.

Plate 197. The Artemis of the Ephesians, a marble statue with bronze head, hands, and feet. *Museo dei Conservatori, Rome.*

Plate 198. Altar dedicated to an unknown god on the Palatine in Rome.

Plates 194–6. In the footsteps of St Paul. 194: entry gate to the 'Street called Straight' in Damascus, the *Cardo maximus* which formed the main street in all Graeco-Roman towns. The little gate is really the side gate of the monumental entry, of which the main arch was to the left. 195: the Lechaion way in Corinth, often travelled by St Paul. 196: Antioch on the Orontes; from the ruins of the citadel modern Antakya can be seen. Apart from a few ruins it retains no trace of the glittering capital of the Seleucids but the name. Antioch was once one of the most important centres for the propagation of the Christian message.

Plate 199. Detail from a relief on the inner side of the triumphal arch of Titus on the Forum in Rome. Romans wearing wreaths bear in triumph the massive seven-branched candlestick from the destroyed temple of Jerusalem.

further organization of his communities and charges these helpers with the preservation of the doctrine he has preached. He was beheaded in Rome probably *c.* A.D. 67; Peter had probably been martyred earlier.

By this time, however, Christianity had already obtained a firm hold within the Roman empire. Paul used by preference to work in the largest centres like Ephesus, the most important junction of sea and land routes on the coast of Asia Minor. There the silver-smiths had rightly exclaimed that their great Artemis, the lewd goddess with her many breasts, would be 'deposed from her magnificence' (Ac 19.27; see Plate 197) if Paul were left in peace. In the place of these and other divinities, including the unknown gods which the people worshipped for fear some should be neglected (Ac 17.23; see Plate 198), Christianity proclaimed the God of Israel whose Temple in Jerusalem had been given up to destruction (Plate 199) because now, in Jesus His Son, He sought to take up His abode in the hearts of all mankind.

Acknowledgements

Agence Rapho, Paris: Plates 164–5
Alinari, Florence: 144–5, 149, 192, 197–9
Allegro, Manchester: 55–6, 166
Arab Legion Air Force, 'Ammân: 30, 65–6, 92, 156, 159, 179
Archives Photographiques, Paris: 91 (centre and right), 148
British Museum, London: 60, 121
Brown, E. E.: 106
Consulate of Israel, Amsterdam: 4
Creten, Canon J., Louvain: 77
Department of Antiquities, 'Ammân: 27, 52 (fifth seal), 57 (right)
Department of Antiquities, Israel: 52 (top right)
Dunand, Maurice, Beirut: 24
École Biblique et Archéologique Française, Jerusalem: 69–71, 78, 188
Elia Photo Service, Jerusalem: 105
Elsevier, N.V. Uitgeversmaatschappij, Amsterdam: 73, 131, 136–7, 146,
    181, 195
Eyckeler, J., Druten: 169
Galloway, E., New York: 178
Giegel, Zurich: 168, 172
Giraudon, Paris: 49 (third row, right)
Grollenberg Collection: 3, 18
Grollenberg, L., O.P.: 6, 8–10, 12, 19–22, 26, 28, 31–4, 35 (left row,
    bottom row, and vessels 2, 4, 5, 6), 36, 42, 48, 49 (top), 51, 52 (bottom
    right), 63–4, 80, 83, 88, 103, 114, 119, 129–30, 132, 140, 146, 152–3,
    155, 157, 158, 160–63, 170, 175, 177, 185, 193–4, 196
Hendrikse, P. (for data supplied to the author): 102, 187
Illustrated London News, London: 49 (bottom row), 93 (left figure), 96–7
Institut Français d'Archéologie, Beirut: 1, 11, 14–17, 25, 154
Israel Information Service, New York: 94, 180

Keren Hayesod, Jerusalem: 176
Koninklijk Kabinet van Munten en Penningen en gesneden Steden, The Hague: 49 (third row, left), 141, 143, 147
Laxague, H.D., o.p., Oullins: 81, 150
Lelong, P., Paris: 186
Lloyd, Dr Seton, Ankara: 58
Louvre, Musée du, Paris: 46–7, 50 (left), 126–7
Maliepaard, Ir. C. H. J., The Hague: 61
Mansell Collection, London: 122, 124–5, 133
Matson Photo Service, Los Angeles: 79, 104, 128, 173–4
Oriental Institute, Chicago: 90
Pennarts and Glissenaar, Montfoort: 62, 93, 120
Ploeg, Dr J. van der, o.p.: 184
Poll, W. van de, Amsterdam: 2, 29, 67
Popper, Paul, London: 89, 183, 191
Pritchard, J. B., Berkeley, California: 53–4, 84, 98–9
Rijksmuseum voor Oudheden, Leiden: 41, 43, 44 (palettes), 45, 74, 115
Rockefeller Museum, Jerusalem: 35 (pottery vessels 1 and 3), 37–8, 40, 49 (second row), 50 (right), 52 (left, and centre right, 4 seals), 57 (centre and foot), 100, 111, 112 (top and foot), 117, 135 (spoon), 151, 167
Schweig, Jerusalem: 23
Spaarnestad, Messrs, Haarlem: 5, 7
Stroete, P. G. te, Nijmegen: 171, 182
The Times, London: 82
Yadin, Y., Jerusalem: 86–7, 107–8, 118

Illustrations from Books

The Biblical Archaeologist, New Haven, Connecticut: Plates 57 (top), 109
Kraeling, E. G., *The Brooklyn Museum Aramaic Papyri*, New Haven, Connecticut, 1953: 139
Bruin, P., and Giegel, P., *Hier hat Gott Gelebt*, Zurich: 168, 172
Legrain, *Status et Statuettes*: 95
Loud, G., and Altman, C. B., *Khorsabad*, Part II, Chicago, 1938: 123
McCown, *Tell en-Nasbe*: 101
The Megiddo Expedition, Megiddo II: 113
Reigenberg, A., *Ancient Jewish Coins*, Jerusalem, 1947: 135 (coin)
Schubart, W., *Papyri Graeci Berolinenses*: 44 (papyrus)
Thureau-Dangin, F., Barrois, A., Dossing, G., and Dunand, M., *Arslân-Tash*, Paris, 1932: 112 (centre)

Torczyner, H., Harding, L., and others, *Lachish I – The Lachish Letters*, London, 1938: 85

Unger, E., *Babylon*, Leipzig, 1931: 134

Vigouroux, F., *Dictionnaire de la Bible*, Paris, 1895–1912: 72, 75–6

Wreszinski, *Atlas zur altägyptischen Kulturgeschichte*, Leipzig, 1923: 13

The author's grateful thanks are due to P. B. Bagatti, O.F.M. (for Plates 39 and 189–90), and P. M. E. Boismard (both of Jerusalem), R. J. Demarée (The Hague), Madame Desroches-Noblecourt (Paris), Dr R. Frankena (Leiden), Dr J. van der Ploeg, O.P., P. Jean-Roger, A.A. (Jerusalem), Dr A. A. Kampman (Leiden), J. B. Pritchard (Berkeley, California), Dr W. D. van Wijngaarden (Leiden), and Y. Yadin (Jerusalem) for their kind co-operation in obtaining and interpreting some of the photographs.

Indexes

BIBLICAL REFERENCES

GENESIS (Gn)

1	82, 179
10	77
10.6	31
10.18	75
11.3	43
11.18–26	98
12–50	89, 92
14.18–24	141
15.6	92
17	92, 179
18, 19	101
19.30–38	91
22.20–24	127
25.13–16	127
25.22–6	91
30.37	101

EXODUS (Ex)

12.38	110
13.1–16	87
25–31	179
35–40	179

LEVITICUS (Lv) — 179

NUMBERS (Num)

11.4	110
13.16	123

DEUTERONOMY (Dt)

6.4–9	87
11.13–21	87
11.14	39
25.4	172
26.5–10	89
34.1–8	82

JOSHUA (Jos)

3.16	21
11.10	117
13–21	77
13.27	77
15	118
17.11–13	118
21.45	116
23.15	116
24	119

JUDGES (Jg)

1.27–35	118
2.6–3.4	126
5	127
5.19	80
10.6–16	126

2 SAMUEL (2 S)

2.13	81
5.8	135
7	133
8	133
9–20	133
12.28	135
16.5	137
20.1	148

1 KINGS (1 K)

1–2	133
3.4	114
4.7–20	145
4.29–34	145
5.18	45
6.29	143
9.15	118
11	148

1 Kings *cont.*

12.16	148
13–14	150

2 KINGS (2 K)

14.7	193
17	150
20.20	131
25.14	173
25.23	79

1 CHRONICLES (1 Ch)

11.6	135

2 CHRONICLES (2 Ch)

25.12	193

EZRA

1.7	173

PSALMS (Ps)

2.7	131
89	133
110.1	131
132	133

PROVERBS (Pr)

1–9	181
10–22	145, 181
25–9	145, 181

ISAIAH (Is)

5.11–14	87
5.24–5	87
5.26–9	171
7.17	150
10.9	Map 7
10.28–34	171
13.12	78
21.10	172
24–7	179
28.21	135
30, 31	193
40–55	169
40.1	87
54.11–12	87

JEREMIAH (Jer)

13.4–7	172
30.18	49
39.3	71
42.1	78

EZEKIEL (Ezk)

27.9	45
29.10	181
30.6	181
34.16	213
38–9	179

DANIEL (Dn)

11.20	191
11.30	191

AMOS (Am)

3.15	143
6.4	143

2 MACCABEES (2 Mac)

3.7ff.	191

MATTHEW (Mt)

2.22	215
2.23	Map 9
4.13	Map 9
16.13	Map 9
23.5	87
27.57	Map 9

MARK (Mk)

6.14–29	Map 9

LUKE (Lk)

2.49	223
3.1	219
7.11	Map 9
19.12, 14	215
24.13	Map 9

JOHN (Jn)

1.28	224
2.1	39, Map 9
3.23	224, Map 9
4	Map 9
11.54	Map 9

ACTS (Ac)

2–4	237
8.26	Map 9
8.40	Map 9
9	239
9–11	Map 9
9.32	Map 9
9.35	Map 9

10	237, Map 9
13	237
17.23	244
19.27	244
21.7	Map 9
22	239

23.31	Map 9
26	239

2 CORINTHIANS (2 Co)

11.32	193

PERSONS, PLACES, AND THINGS

Pages which include plates are in *italic* type

Abel-beth-maacah,	Map 6	Akeldama,	Map 5
Abel-keramim,	Map 4	Akhenaton,	105, 129
Abel-meholah,	Maps 4, 6	'Aqir,	81
Abel-shittim,	Map 4	Alalakh,	Map 3
Abijam,	164	Albinus,	217
Abila,	Map 9	Aleppo,	Maps 1, 3
Abisar,	101	Alexander the Great,	33, 35, 179,
Abraham,	89–98, 213, 214, Map 3		183, *185*, Map 7
Accad,	Map 1	Alexander Jannaeus,	186, *187*, 195
Accadians,	67	Alexandria,	182, 183, 184, Maps 1, 8
Acco,	42, *163*, 188, Maps 2, 3, 6	Alexandrium,	Map 9
Achaia,	Map 10	Almon,	166
Achmetha,	Map 1	Alphabet,	47, 77
Achshaph,	Map 4	Altar,	*140*
Actium,	197	Amanus,	Map 3
Acts,	217, 237–9	Amarna archives,	117
Adad-nirari III,	157, 164	Amaziah,	164, 193
Adam (man),	146	Ambibulus, Marcus,	216
Adam (place),	21, Map 4	Amenophis I,	105
Admah,	Map 3	Amenophis III,	77, 103
Adonai,	85	Amenophis IV,	63, 77, 105
Adoni-ner,	79	Amminadab,	79
Adoraim,	Map 6	'Ammân,	Map 2
Adramyttium,	Map 10	Ammon,	91, 98, 153, Maps 4, 6, 7
Adullam,	Maps 4, 6	Ammon, Oasis of,	Map 8
Aenon,	224	Ammonites,	127
Agrippa I,	215, 216, 219	Amon,	*129*, 131
Agrippa II,	217, 219	Amon (King of Judah),	165
Ahab, King,	118, 143, 151, 155, 163,	Amos,	164, 167, 171
	164	Amphipolis,	Map 10
Ahaz,	165	*Amrît*,	54
Ahaziah,	164	Amygdalon,	Map 5
Ahijah,	148, 164	Anab,	Map 4
Ai,	113, 120, 123, Map 4	'Anâta,	172, *168*
Aiath,	166	Anathoth,	137, 169, 172
Aijalon,	Maps 4, 6	Ancyra (*Ankara*),	Maps 1, 8

Andrew,	233	Asphalt Lake,	Map 9
Annius Rufus,	216	Assos,	Map 10
Antakya,	*242*	Assuân,	*180*, 181
Antigonus,	195	Assyria,	155–60, Maps 1, 7
Anti-Lebanon,	19, Map 3	Assyrians,	164–5, 193
Antioch,	183, 213, *242*, Maps 1, 10	Ataroth,	Map 6
Antioch (in Pisidia),	Map 10	Athaliah,	164
Antiochus III,	*185*, 188, 191	Athens,	191, 213, Maps 1, 8, 10
Antiochus IV,	*187*, 188, 191	Aton,	63
Antipater,	195	Attalia,	Map 10
Antipatris,	Map 9	Augustus,	197, 215, 216
Antonia,	Map 5	Azekah,	Maps 4, 6
Apamea,	182	Azariah,	158
Aphek, later Antipatris,	Maps 4, 6	Azotus,	Map 9
Aphek (in Asher),	Map 4		
Aphek (in Transjordan),	Map 6	Baal,	74, 149, 163, 197
Aphrodite,	186	Ba'albek,	*196*, 197, Map 3
Apollo,	186	Baal-hazor,	37, Map 2
'Aqaba,	18	Baal-meon,	Map 6
Arabah,	18, 21	Baal-perazim,	135
Arad,	Map 4	Baal-shalishah,	Map 6
Arados,	182	Baal-shamem,	188
Aram-naharaim,	98, Map 3	Baal-zephon,	110
Araunah,	137, 141, Map 5	Baasha,	164
Arbela,	Map 1	Babel, Tower of,	*175*
Archelaus,	215, 216	Babylon,	15, 31, 169, 173, *175*, 177, 183,
Aretas IV, King,	193		Maps 1, 7, 8
Arimathea,	Map 9	Babylonia,	181, Maps 1, 7, 8
Aristobulus,	193, 195	Baghdad,	31, Map 1
Ark of the Covenant,	127, 137, 139	*Bahr Lût*,	98
Armenia,	33, Map 8	Bahurim,	137
Arnon,	39, 111, *112*, Maps 2, 6	Baibars,	45
Aroer,	Maps 4, 6	*Balîkh*,	Map 3
Arpad,	Map 7	Barak,	80, 127, 223, Map 4
Arqa,	Map 3	Barnabas,	Map 10
Arslân-Tash,	74, 143, Map 1	Baruch,	78, 173
Artemis,	*243*, 244	Bashan,	Map 2
Arubboth,	Map 6	Beeroth,	166, Map 4
Arumah,	Map 4	Beer-sheba,	Maps 2, 3, 4, 6, 9
Arvad,	35, 54, 75, 182, Map 3	*Behistun*,	67, Map 1
Asa,	164	Beirut,	Map 1
Ashdod,	Maps 2, 4, 6, 7, 9	*Beisân*,	80
Asher,	Map 4	*Beit Sahûr*,	227
Ashkelon,	182, Maps 2, 4, 6, 9	*Beni-hasan*,	101, Map 1
Ashtaroth,	158, Map 3	Benjamin,	Map 4
Ashur,	Maps 1, 7	Beqa',	19, 197, 215
Ashurbanipal,	157, *158*, 160, *161*, 165	Beroea,	Map 10
Ashurdan III,	164	Berytus,	182
Ashurnasirpal III,	164	Beth-anath,	Map 4
Ashur-nirari,	164	Bethany (nr Jerusalem),	236, Map 9
Asia (province),	Map 10	Bethany (trans-Jordan),	224

256

Beth-arbel, Map 6
Bethel, 101, 120, 148–9, 166, Maps 4, 6
Bethesda, Map 5
Beth-ezel, Map 6
Beth-gamul, Map 6
Beth-haggan, Map 6
Beth-horon, Maps 4, 6
Beth-jeshimoth, Map 4
Bethlehem (in Judah), 80, 131, 214, 220, 227, Maps 2, 3, 4, 6, 9
Bethlehem (in Zebulun), Map 4
Bethphage, 137
Beth-saida, 230, Map 9
Beth-shan, 41, 42, 57, 74, 80, 126, 141, 182, Maps 2, 3, 6
Beth-shemesh, Map 6
Beth-shittah, Map 4
Beth-zatha, Map 5
Beth-zur, Map 6
Bezabde, 33
Bezek, Map 6
Bisutun, 67, Map 1
Bithynia, Map 10
Boghaz-Keui, Map 1
Bozra, Maps 3, 7
Brick-bakers, 106–7
Busra, Map 3
Byblos, 28, 31, 44, 45, 182, Maps 3, 7, 8

Caesarea, 213, Maps 2, 9, 10
Caesarea Philippi, 233, Map 9
Caiaphas' dwelling, Map 5
Cairo, Map 1
Calah, 155, Map 1
Caligula, 215, 216
Calno, Map 7
Calvary, 137, 236
Cambyses, 165
Camel, 15
Cana, Map 9
Canaan, 31, 75, 98, Map 3
Capernaum, 230–33, Maps 2, 9
Caponius, 216
Carchemish, Maps 1, 3, 7
Caria, Map 10
Carmel, Mount, 39, 111, 153, 162, 163, 171, 223, Maps 2, 4, 6
Carmel (in Judah), Map 6
Cassius Longinus, 217
Cauda, Map 10
Cedars, 29, 30, 31, 137

Cenacle, 137
Cenchreae, Map 10
Cestius Gallus, 217
Chalcis, 215, 219
Chaldaeans, 165, 173, Map 7
Champollion, J. F., 61–2
Chephirah, Map 4
Cherubim, 143, 146
Chinnereth, Maps 4, 6
Chios, Map 10
Chnumhotep, 100, 101
Chorazin, 230, Map 9
Chronicles, 85, 151
Chronicler, 179
Cilicia, 155, 239, Maps 7, 8, 10
Cilician Gates, 239
Cizre, 31, 33, Map 1
Claudius, 215–19
Clay nails, 71
Cleopatra, 187, 197
Cnidus, Map 10
Coins, 176, 184, 185, 187
Colossae, Map 10
Colossians, 241
Colossians, Epistle to the, 217, Map 10
Commodus, 184
Corbulo, 217
Corinth, 242, Map 10
Corinthians, Epistles to the, 217, Map 10
Cos, Map 10
Crete, 127, Maps 7, 8, 10
Cuneiform writing, 65, 67, 68, 69
Cuspius Fadus, 216
Cyprus, 35, 141, Maps 1, 10
Cyrene, Map 1
Cyrus, 165, 177–9, Map 1

Dalmanutha, 233
Damascus, 153, 155, 182, 213, 241, Maps 1, 3, 7, 8
Dan, 149, Maps 2, 3, 6
Daniel (book), 177, 188–9
Darius I, 67, 165, 179
David, 71, 91, 129–37, 141, 146, 148, 164, 193, 213
Dead, Book of the, 64, 65
Dead Sea, 18, 36, 37, 99, 101, 193, 198, 199, 200, 201, Maps 2, 9
Debir, Map 4
Deborah, 127, Map 4

257

Decapolis,	Map 9
Delta of the Nile,	22, 101, 103
Denderah,	186, Map 1
Deportation policy,	160, 167, 169
Derbe,	Map 10
Deutero-Isaiah,	165, 171, 177
Deuteronomy,	111
Diadochi,	183
Diana,	Map 10
Diaspora (Dispersion),	181, 239
Dibon,	53, 241, Maps 2, 6
Dispersion,	181, 239
Dominus Flevit,	57, 137, Map 5
Domitian,	217
Dor,	Maps 3, 4, 6
Dothan,	*50*, 53, Maps 2, 3, 6
Dur Sharrukin,	*157*, 160
Ebal,	37, Map 4
Ecbatana,	Maps 1, 8
Ecclesiastes,	145, 188
Ecclesiasticus,	188
Edfu,	43, *186*
Edom,	153, Map 7
Edomites,	21, 91, 213
Edrei,	Map 3
Eglon,	81
Egypt,	22, 31, Maps 1, 7
Ehud,	127, Map 4
Ekron,	81, Maps 2, 6
Elah,	164
El-Amarna,	63, 77, Map 1
Elam,	Map 6
Elamites,	67
Elath,	18, 141, Map 7
El-Balu'a,	74
Elealeh,	Map 6
Elephantine,	43, 180, 181
Elijah,	153, 155, 157, 164, 223
Elisha,	153, 155, 163, 164
El-Jib,	81, *114*
El-Muqanna',	81
Eltekeh,	81
Emesa,	Map 8
Emmaus,	Map 9
En-dor,	126, Map 6
En-gedi,	Map 6
En-rogel,	Map 5
Entemena,	71
Ephesians, Epistle to the,	217
Ephesus,	244, Maps 1, 8, 10

Ephraim,	37, 148, 150, Maps 2, 4
Ephron,	Map 6
Erech,	71, Map 1
Esarhaddon,	165, Map 7
Esau,	89, 91
Esdraelon,	224
Eshtaol,	Map 4
Eshtemoa,	Map 6
Essenes,	199, 211
Esther (book),	181
Etham,	Map 6
Ethnarch,	215
Et-Tell,	123
Euphrates,	31, *32*, 33, 172, 175, Maps 1, 3, 8
Eusebius,	77
Evil-merodach,	165
Excavation,	51–9
Ezekiel,	165, 169, 177
Ezion-geber,	16, 141
Ezra,	165, 179
Ezra (book),	85, 177
Fair Havens,	Map 10
Fashkha Spring,	198, 211
Felix, Antonius,	217, Map 10
Festus, Porcius,	217, Map 10
Flinders Petrie, W.,	51
Forum of Appius,	Map 10
Gabbatha,	236, Map 5
Gad,	164
Gadara,	Map 9
Galatia,	241, Map 10
Galatians (book),	217, Map 10
Galba,	217
Galilee,	223–6, Maps 2, 9
Galilee, Sea of,	17, 226, *228–9*, Map 2
Gallim,	166
Gallio,	Map 10
Gamaliel,	239
Gath,	Maps 4, 6
Gath-hepher,	Map 6
Gaugamela,	33, Map 8
Gaulanitis,	Map 9
Gaza,	51, 182, Maps 2, 3, 4, 6, 8, 9
Geba,	124, 128, 166, Maps 2, 6
Gebal	45, Map 3
Gebim,	166
Gehenna,	Map 5
Ge-hinnom,	Map 5

258

Gennesaret, Lake of, Map 9
Gerar, Maps 3, 6
Gerasa, Maps 2, 9
Gerizim, Mount, 37, *94, 96–7*, Maps 4, 9
Geshur, Map 6
Gessius Florus, 217
Gethsemane, Garden of, 137, 236, Map 5
Gezer, 51, 135, Maps 2, 3, 4, 6
Gibbethon, Map 6
Gibeah, 166, Maps 4, 6
Gibeon, 41, 80, 81, 113, 114, *115, 130,* 135, 166, Maps 2, 4, 6
Giblet, 45
Gideon, 127, Map 4
Gihon, Spring, 131, 135, 137, Map 5
Gilboa, 39, *126,* 128, 129, 223, Maps 2, 6
Gilead, 155, Map 2
Gilgal (in Ephraim), Map 6
Gilgal (in Benjamin), 127, Maps 4, 6
Gimzo, Map 6
Gobryas, 71
Golgotha, Map 5
Gomorrah, Map 3
Gordium, Map 8
Goshen, Land of, 107
Gospels, 215–22
Gozan, Map 7
Gozarta, 33
Grotefend, 67
Gubla, 45

Habor, 33
Hadad, *74*
Hadadezer, 155
Haggai, 165, 171, 179
Haifa, *162,* 171, Map 2
Ham, 31, Map 3
Hamanu, 157
Hamath (*Hama*), *46,* 47–9, Maps 1, 3, 7
Hammurabi, 33, *68,* 69
Hannibal, 191
Haran (*Harrân*), 91, 95, 98, Maps 1, 3, 7
Harosheth-ha-goiim, Map 4
Harp player, 144
Hasmonaeans, 193, 195, 214, Map 5
Hathor, 186
Hatshepsut, 26, *62–3,* 131, 145

Hattushash, Map 1
Hazael, 143
Hazazon-tamar, Map 3
Hazor, 53, 113, *117, 118,* 120, *138,* 139, 141, 149, Maps 2, 3, 4, 6
Hebrews, 105–10
Hebron, 37, 101, 129, *212,* 214, Maps 2, 3, 4, 6
Hecatompylos Map 8
Heliodorus, 191
Helios, 197
Hepher, Maps 4, 6
Hermon, Mount, 18, *19,* 111, 233, Map 3
Herod Antipas, 215, 216, 226
Herod the Great, 139, 195–7, 213–14, 215, 216
Herodium, 49, 214, 226, Map 9
Heshbon, 80, Maps 4, 6
Hezekiah, 131, 135, 150, 165
Hieratic script, 63
Hieroglyphs, 61–2
Highways, 41–2
Hill Country, Map 4
Hinnom, Valley of, Map 5
Hippos, Map 9
Hittites, 35, 69, 71, 77, 105, Map 1
Hophra (Apries), 165
Horemheb, 104, 105
Horus, 65, 186
Hosea (prophet), 164, 167–9
Hoshea (Joshua), 123
Hoshea (King of Israel), 165
Huldah, 165
Huleh, Lake, Map 2
Hyksos, 103–5
Hyrcanium, *48,* 214
Hyrcanus, John, 49, 193, 195, 201

Ibleam, Map 6
Ibsha, 101, 103
Iconium, Map 10
Idols, *124*
Idumaea, Map 9
Idumaeans, 193
Ilium, Map 8
India, 183
Iran, 33
Irpeel, 166
Isaiah, 92, 149–50, 160, 165, 169, 171, 191

Ishmael,	127
Ishtar,	155
Israel,	148, 150, 151
Issachar,	Map 4
Issus,	182, Map 8
Istanbul,	Map 1
Ituraeans,	193
Ivory carving,	*142*
Jabbok,	20, 39, *93*, 95, 101, Maps 2, 6
Jabesh-gilead,	Maps 4, 6
Jabneel,	Map 6
Jacob,	89, 91, 103, 148
Jacob's Well,	95, Map 9
Jaffa,	Map 2
Jahaz,	Map 4
Jamnia,	Map 9
Jarmuth,	Map 4
Jattir,	Map 6
Jazer,	Map 6
Jeba',	*125*
Jebeil,	*44*, 45
Jebel Músa,	*108*
Jehoahaz,	165
Jehoiachin,	165
Jehoiakim,	165
Jehoshaphat,	164
Jehu, King,	155, 163, 164
Jehud,	177
Jephthah,	127, Map 4
Jeremiah,	78, 165, 166, 169, 171, 172, 173, 177
Jericho,	53, *113*, 120–23, Maps 2, 3, 4, 6, 9
Jeroboam I,	148–50, 164
Jeroboam II,	157, 164, 167
Jerusalem,	80, 81, *129–46*, Maps 1–10
Jesanah,	Map 6
Jesus of Nazareth,	177, 214, 216, 219–22, 223–36 *passim*, 237–44 *passim*
Jezíret Ibn Omar,	33
Jezreel,	126, Map 6
Jezreel, Plain of,	39, 41, *126*, 223, *224*, Map 2
Joahaz,	164
Joash,	164
Job (book),	181
Joel (book),	179
John (Gospel and Epistles),	217, 219, 221
John the Baptist,	87, 216, 223–6
Jokneam,	Maps 4, 6
Jonah,	164, 179
Jonathan Maccabaeus,	189, 193, 199
Joppa,	182, Maps 3, 6, 9
Joram,	164
Jordan (river and valley),	17–19, *20*, 111–13, *225*, *226*, Maps 2, 9
Joseph,	103
Joseph of Arimathea,	Map 5
Josephus, Flavius,	193, 199, 211, 217, 223
Joshua,	111–19 *passim*, 123, Map 4
Joshua (book),	85, 111–14
Josiah,	114, 124, 150, 165, 169, 177, 193
Jotham,	165
Judaea,	Map 9
Judah,	118, 119, 148–51, Maps 2, 4
Judas Maccabaeus,	189
Judges,	124–7
Judges (book),	85, 124–7
Julias,	230, Map 9
Jupiter,	197
Justinian,	109
Kabul	Map 6
Kadesh,	110, 111
Kadesh (on the Orontes),	Map 3
Kafr Kenna,	*38*, 39, *218*, Map 9
Kaftor,	127
Kamon,	Map 4
Karnak,	26, 43, Map 1
Kedesh,	Maps 4, 6
Kenyon, Miss K.,	123
Khábúr,	33, 71
Khirbet Qumrân,	53, 85, 87, *198–211*, Maps 2, 9
Khorsabad,	160, Maps 1, 7
Kidron valley,	*40*, *135*, 139, *232*, 236, Map 5
Kings,	85, 150–51
Kir-hareseth,	Map 6
Kiriathaim, Plain of,	Map 3
Kiriath-jearim,	137, Map 4
Kir-moab,	Map 6
Koinè Greek,	239
Lachish,	78, 79, 81, 113, *116*, 120, 173, Maps 2, 4, 6
Lagash,	31, 71, Map 1
Laishah,	166
Laodicea,	Map 10

260

Larsa,	Map 1
Lasea,	Map 10
Law, The,	82–3, 179, 199
Lebanon,	19, 45, 137, Map 3
Lebo-hamath,	Map 3
Lebonah,	Map 4
Leviticus,	179
Libnah,	Maps 4, 6
Lithostroton,	Map 5
Lot,	91, 98
Lowland,	39, Map 4
Luke,	217, 219, 221, 237, 239
Luxor,	26, 43, 102, Map 1
Lycaonia,	Map 10
Lycia,	Map 10
Lydda,	Map 9
Lydia,	Map 10
Lysanias,	219
Lystra,	Map 10
Maat,	62, 65
Maccabees,	189, 191–3
Macedonia,	Maps 1, 8, 10
Machaerus,	48, 214, 226, Map 9
Madaba,	241
Madmenah,	166
Madon,	Map 4
Magadan,	233
Magdala,	Map 9
Magnesia,	191, Map 1
Mahanaim,	Maps 3, 6
Makaz,	Map 6
Makkedah,	Map 4
Malachi,	179
Malta,	Map 10
Manasseh (tribe),	148
Manasseh (King of Judah),	165
Maon,	Map 6
Marcellus,	216
Marduk,	177
Mareshah,	Map 6
Mari,	32, 117, Map 1
Mark (Gospel),	217, 219
Mark,	221, Map 10
Mar Saba,	41, Map 9
Marullus,	216
Masada,	214, Map 9
Matthew (Gospel),	217, 219
Matthew,	221
Medeba,	241, Map 6
Medes,	189, Map 7
Media,	Map 8
Megiddo,	42, 53, 120, 135, 141, 143, 146, Maps 2, 3, 4, 6
Mekal,	74
Melchizedek,	141
Memphis,	22, 24–5, 43, 105, Maps 1, 7, 8
Menahem,	165
Mendes,	182
Menes,	22
Mephaath,	Map 6
Merom,	113, Map 4
Meroz,	Map 4
Mesha,	153–4
Mesopotamia,	31–3, 43, 191, Map 8
Messiah,	137, 219–21
Michmash,	124, 128, 166
Middle Kingdom,	71
Migdol,	110
Migron,	166
Miletus,	Maps 8, 10
Minet el-Beida,	75
Minnith,	Map 4
Misrephoth-maim,	Map 4
Mitanni,	71, 77
Mizpah,	133, 166, Maps 2, 4, 6
Mizpah of Gilead,	Maps 3, 4
Moab,	74, 91, 98, 111, 127, 153–5, Maps 2, 4, 6
Moph,	24–5
Moreh, Hill of,	Map 4
Moresheth,	Map 6
Moses,	82–3, 105–10 passim, 111, 123, 171
Mount of Offence,	134, Map 5
Mount of Olives,	171, 236, Map 5
Mucianus,	217
Mukhmás,	124
Mycenaean pottery,	54
Myra,	Map 10
Mysia,	Map 10
Nabataeans,	195, Map 9
Nabonidus,	165
Nabopolassar,	165
Nabuchodonosor,	71
Nadab,	164
Nag Hammadi,	Map 1
Nahor,	127
Nahum,	165
Nain,	126, Map 9

Nathan, 133, 137, 164, 166
Naucratis, 182
Nazareth, 39, 223, *224*, Maps 2, 9
Neapolis, Map 10
Nebi Samwíl, 41, 114
Nebo, Mount, 111, *112*
Nebuchadnezzar, 71, 165, 173, 175, 177
Necho, 165
Negeb, *21*, 101, Map 3
Nehemiah, 165, 179
Nehemiah (book), 85, 179
Nephtoah, 166
Nergal-sharezer, 71, 165
Nero, 217, 219
Nerva, 165
Netophah, Map 6
New Kingdom, 71
Nile, 22, *23*, 31, *180*, Map 1
Nimrûd, 155
Nineveh, 157, Maps 1, 7
Nippur, 31, Map 1
No-Amon, 26
Nob, 137, 171–2
Nomads, *92*
Noph, *24–5*
Nuzi, Map 1

Obadiah, 179
Obelisks, *28*, *60*, 61, 62, 155
Octavian, 195, 197
Oil lamps, *55*, 58
Old Kingdom, 71
Omri, 151, 153, 154, 164
Ophel, Map 5
Opis, Map 8
Ornan (Araunah), 137–9, 141, Map 5
Orontes, 19, *46*, 47, 183, Map 3
Osiris, 65
Ossuaria, *56*, *234–5*
Ostraca, *78–9*

Paddan-aram, 98
Palmyra, *194*, *196*, 197, Map 8
Pamphylia, Map 10
Paneion, 182
Paphos, Map 10
Papyrus, 45, 63, 181
Parables, 223
Parah, 166, *168*
Parthia, Map 8
Parthians, 195, 197, 201

Patara, Map 10
Patenemheb, 145
Patriarchs, 89–101 *passim*
Paul, St, 217, 219, 237, 239–44, Map 10
Pavement, the, 236, Map 5
Pekah, 165
Pekahiah, 165
Pella (in Palestine), Maps 3, 9
Pella (in Macedonia), Map 8
Pelusium, 110, 182
Peniel, 101
Pentateuch, 82–3, 85, 89–91, 119
Penuel or Peniel, 42, 101, Maps 2, 3, 4, 6
Peraea, 233, 236, Map 9
Perath, 172
Perga, Map 10
Pergamum, Maps 8, 10
Persepolis, 67, *178*, 181, 183, Map 8
Persia, Map 1
Persians, 165
Peter, 216, 217, 219, 233, 237, 244
Pethor, Map 3
Petra, 21, *192*, 195
Petronius, 216
Pharisees, 193, 195, 236
Pharos, 183, *184*
Philadelphia, 182, 188, Map 9
Philadelphia (in Asia), Map 10
Philemon, Map 10
Philemon (Epistle), 217
Philip (tetrarch), 215, 216, 219, 230
Philippi, Map 10
Philippians, Epistle to the, 217, Map 10
Philistia, Map 2
Philistines, 123, 127–8, 129, 135, Maps 4, 6
Philo, 199, 211
Phoenix, Map 10
Phylactery, 87
Pi-hahiroth, 110
Pirathon, Maps 4, 6
Pisidia, Map 10
Plain, Sea of the, *36*, Map 6
Pliny, 199
Pompey, 195
Pontius Pilate, 216
Pontus, Map 10
Popilius Laenas, 191
Pottery, *55*, 57–8

Praetorium, Map 5
Prophets, 163–72
Psalms, 181
Ptolemais, 182, 188, Maps 9, 10
Ptolemies, 183, 188, 191, Map 1
Ptolemy I, *185*
Ptolemy II, 184
Ptolemy III, *187*
Ptolemy VI, 186
Punon, Map 3
Puteoli, Map 10
Pyramids, 58

Qarqar, 151, 155, 164, Maps 3, 7
Qatna, Map 3
Quintilius Varus, 216
Quirinius, 216
Qumrân: see *Khirbet Qumrân*

Rabbah of the Ammonites, 182, 188,
Map 6
Ramah, 166, Map 6
Ramathaim, Map 6
Rameses II, 77, *102*, 105
Rameses III, 123, 127
Ramoth-gilead, 155, Maps 2, 6
Raphia, 182
Râs Shamra, 35, 75–7, Map 3
Rawlinson, Sir Henry, 67–9
Red Sea, 18, 103, 110, 113, Map 1
Reeds, Sea of, 110
Rehob, Map 4
Rehoboam, 151, 164
Rehoboth, Map 3
Rekhmire, 106
Rephaim, Valley of, Map 5
Retenu, 129
Revelation (book), 217
Rezeph, Map 7
Rhegium, Map 10
Rhodes, 213, Maps 1, 10
Rimmon, Map 4
Rogelim, Map 6
Romans, Epistle to the, 217, Map 10
Rome, 191, 195–7, Map 10
Ruâd, *34*

Sadducees, 193, 195, 199
St Catherine, monastery of, 107, *109*
Sais, 182, Map 7
Salamis (on Cyprus), Map 10

Salecah, Map 3
Salim, 224, Map 9
Salt Sea, *36*, Maps 3, 6
Samaria, 42, 53, 78, 151, 153, 182, *212*,
213, 233, Maps 1, 2, 6, 7, 9
Samos, Map 10
Samothrace, Map 10
Samson, 127, Map 4
Samuel, 85, 127–8, 133
Sanhedrin, Map 5
Saphon, 77
Sarcophagus, *56*
Sardis, Maps 8, 10
Sargon II, 157, 160, 165, Map 7
Saul, 128, 129, 133, 163
Scarab seals, *79*
Scipio Africanus, 191
Scythopolis, 182, Map 9
Seals, *72*, *79*
Sebaste, 153, 213, Map 9
Sebastiyeh, 153
Seir, 91
Sela, 193
Seleucia, 182, Map 10
Seleucids, 183, 188, 191, 193, 195, 243,
Map 1
Seleucus IV, 191
Sennacherib, 150, 160, 165, 169, Map 7
Sergius Paulus, Map 10
Sesostris II, 101
Set, 77
Seti I, 31
Sewêne, 181
Shallum, 165
Shalmaneser III, 155, 164
Shalmaneser IV, 164
Shalmaneser V, 151, 160, 165
Shamshi-adad V, 164
Sharon, Plain of, 39, Maps 2, 4, 9
Sharuhen, Map 3
Shechem, 37, 41, 42, 53, 95, 101, 148,
233, Maps 2, 3, 4, 6
Shema, 87
Sheshbazzar, 165, 179
Shiloh, 127, 128, 148, Maps 2, 4, 6
Shimron, Map 4
Shishak (Sheshonq), 150, 164
Shulgi, 71
Shunem, 126, Map 6
Siddim, Valley of, Map 3
Sidon, 182, 233, Maps 3, 8, 10

Silas, Map 10
Siloam, pool of, Map 5
Siloam, tower of, Map 5
Silwân, *134*
Simon Maccabaeus, 189
Sin, Map 3
Sinai, 16, 107, *108–9*, Map 1
Sirach, 188
Smyrna, 191, Maps 1, 10
Socoh, Map 6
Sodom, Map 3
Solomon, 133, 137–46, 148, 164
Stelae, *74*, 75, 153, *154*
Stephen, 216
Street called Straight, 241, *242*
Succoth, *95*, 101, Maps 3, 4, 6
Sultantepe, 90, Map 3
Sumer, 65–7, Map 1
Susa, 181, Maps 1, 7, 8
Sychar, Map 9
Syene, 181
Syracuse, Map 10
Syria, Maps 8, 10
Syrian desert, 15–17, Map 1
Syro-Arabian desert, 15–17, Map 3
Syro-Phoenicia, Map 9
Syrtis, Map 10

Taanach, 53, 80, Maps 2, 3, 6
Tabor, Mount, *38*, 120, *121*, 127, 223, 233, Maps 2, 4, 9
Talmud, 223
Tanis, 182
Tappuah (in Ephraim), Maps 4, 6
Tarsus, 239, Maps 1, 3, 10
Taurus, Maps 3, 8
Tekoa, 167, Map 6
Teleilât el-Ghassûl, Map 2
Tell, 47, 49, *50*, 51–9
Tell Abu Hawâm, Map 2
Tell Beit Mirsim, 120, Map 2
Tell Deir 'Alla, *94*
Tell ed-Dâmiyeh, *21*
Tell ed-Duweir, 81
Tell el-'Ajjûl, 57, Map 2
Tell el-Fâra'ah, Map 2
Tell el-Hesy, 51, 81, Map 2
Tell el-Hosn, 80
Tell el-Qasîleh, 78, Map 2
Tell en-Nasbeh, *133*
Tell Jemmeh, Map 2

Tell Ta'anak, 80
Tell Waqqâs, *117*
Temple (of Herod), 214
Temple (of Solomon), 139, *140*
Temple square, *231*
Tetragram, 85
Tetrarch, 215
Thapsacus, Map 8
Thebes, 22, 26, 62, Map 1
Thebez, Maps 4, 6
Thessalonica, 241, Map 10
Thessalonians, Epistle to the, 217
Thoth, 65
Thothmes III, 63, 75, 77, 117, *129*, 131
Thrace, Maps 8, 10
Three Taverns, Map 10
Thyatira, Map 10
Tiberias, 226, *228–9*, Map 9
Tiberius, 216, 230
Tiberius Alexander, 217
Tiglath-pileser III, 158, 160, 164, 169, Map 7
Tigris, 31, *32*, 33, Maps 1, 8
Timnah, Map 4
Timnath-serah, Map 4
Timothy, Map 10
Timothy, Epistles to, 217
Tirhakah, 164
Tirzah, 37, 42, *52*, 53, 151, *152*, 153, Maps 2, 3, 4, 6
Tishbe, Map 6
Titus, Epistle to, 217, 241
Titus, Arch of, *244*
Trajan, 217
Tripolis, *17*, 19, 45, 182
Troas, Map 10
Tribes of Israel, 126–8
Tutankhamon, 105, 129
Tyre, *34*, 153, 155, 157, 182, 183, 213, 233, Maps 3, 6, 7, 8, 10
Tyropoeon Valley, 137

Ugarit, 33–5, 77, Map 3
Ummidius Quadratus, 217
Unger, E., 175
Ur, 31, 71, *90*, 95, Maps 1, 7
Uriah (prophet), 165, 166
Uruk, 71
Uzziah (Azariah), 158, 164, 167

Valerius Gratus, 216

264

Valley of the Kings, 27
Ventidius Cumanus, 217
Vespasian, 217
Vibius Marsius, 216
Vitellius, 216
Volusius Saturninus, 216

Wâdi Far'ah, 20
Wâdi Muraba'at, 87
Water tunnels, *130*, *132*, 135, Map 5
Wilderness of Judah (Judaea), *40*, 41, 224, *227*, Map 2
Winnowing, *170*, 172
Writing prophets, 164–5, 167–72

Xerxes, 179
Xystos, Map 5

Yahweh, 85, 114–16, 145, 146, 148–50
Yahwism, 171
Yahwistic chronicle, 146
Yahwistic history, 179
Yarmuk, 39, Map 2

Zab, Great, 31
Zab, Little, 31
Zaphon, 77
Zarephath, Map 3
Zebedee, 233
Zeboim, Map 3
Zebulun, Map 4
Zechariah, 165, 171, 179
Zedekiah, 165
Zemar, 75, Map 3
Zemarites, 75
Zephaniah, 165
Zered, Brook, *93*
Zeredah, Map 6
Zerubbabel, 165, 179
Zeus, 186, 188
Ziggurats, 43–5, 73, *90*, *157*, *175*
Zion, 135, 137, Map 5
Ziph, Map 6
Zimri, 164
Zoar, Map 3
Zorah, Maps 4, 6
Zoser, 24

MORE ABOUT PENGUINS, PELICANS AND PUFFINS

For further information about books available from Penguins please write to Dept EP, Penguin Books Ltd, Harmondsworth, Middlesex UB7 0DA.

In the U.S.A.: For a complete list of books available from Penguins in the United States write to Dept DG, Penguin Books, 299 Murray Hill Parkway, East Rutherford, New Jersey 07073.

In Canada: For a complete list of books available from Penguins in Canada write to Penguin Books Canada Ltd, 2801 John Street, Markham, Ontario L3R 1B4.

In Australia: For a complete list of books available from Penguins in Australia write to the Marketing Department, Penguin Books Australia Ltd, P.O. Box 257, Ringwood, Victoria 3134.

In New Zealand: For a complete list of books available from Penguins in New Zealand write to the Marketing Department, Penguin Books (N.Z.) Ltd, P.O. Box 4019, Auckland 10.

In India: For a complete list of books available from Penguins in India write to Penguin Overseas Ltd, 706 Eros Apartments, 56 Nehru Place, New Delhi 110019.

Who's Who in the Ancient World

Betty Radice

Was Keats's Endymion the fellow who . . . or was that
Hyperion? What links *The Family Reunion* with *Les Mouches*
and Strauss's *Elektra*? What was Scipio's triumph? And never
mind the centaurs, *who* were the Lapiths?

Whether we travel in Europe or seek enjoyment in literature, in
art, in opera or at the concert, we are constantly up against
Greek and Latin names, titles and allusions. To meet this
difficulty Betty Radice has compiled this illustrated companion
to the elite of classical antiquity and their most important
appearances in Western art. Her work, which is fully indexed
and cross-referenced, also contains an introduction tracing the
fortunes of our classical legacy from Homer's *Iliad* to such
latter-day works as Picasso's *Vollard Suite* and Cavafy's
Oedipus.

A Dictionary of Saints

Donald Attwater

An alphabetical reference book to the lives and legends of more than 750 saints, from Christ's apostles to the men and women who have been canonized in recent times, with full details of their work, their feast-days, emblems, and dates of canonization.

The author, a Roman Catholic, has specialized for many years in hagiology and carried out the most recent revision of the standard work, Butler's *Lives of the Saints*. Though the records of many saints are necessarily scanty, he has aimed to make this dictionary as historically reliable as possible.

A Dictionary of Modern History
Now revised and updated

A. W. Palmer

This book is intended as a reference-companion to the
personalities, events, and ideas of the last century and a half.
While the prime emphasis is on British affairs and on political
topics, the Dictionary is intended to represent trends in the
history of all the major regions of the world. Particular care has
been taken to include numerous entries on the U.S.A. and on
Russia, areas which earlier books tended to neglect. The entries
are arranged in alphabetical order (with appropriate cross-
references) and are in essay form, ranging in length from little
more than 100 words to nearly 2,000. There are entries on
economic, social, religious and scientific developments, but not
on the arts. Explanations are given of some of the famous
descriptive phrases of the period. About a third of the entries
are biographical.

The book is intended as an aid to study, and not a substitute for
it. The author hopes that it will explain the passing allusion and
stimulate an interest in unfamiliar facets of historical
knowledge.

The Penguin Atlas of Ancient History
The Penguin Atlas of Medieval History
The Penguin Atlas of Modern History

Colin McEvedy

These three volumes carry the story of European history
forward from the dawn of time to the battle of Waterloo.
Explanatory notes facing each map deal with the major events
of the period covered. Exceptionally clearly drawn and lettered,
these books will be a boon for anyone interested in history of
the wider sort, but who can never remember where the Gepids
(a German tribe of the Dark Ages) lived prior to A.D. 406, or
whether the Danes were protestant or catholic in the sixteenth
century.